Advance Praise for *Pilgrimage through Loss*

"Linda Lawrence Hunt's *Pilgrimage through Loss* is an important book, especially for any family devastated by the death of a child. I know parents need the encouragement and help offered here because I lost my son, Spencer. All who read this will be blessed!"
—DR. JOHN PERKINS, Author and Founder of Mendenhall Ministries

"Having recently lost my mother, I am particularly grateful right now for authentic stories from people who have journeyed through grief toward healing. Linda Hunt's mix of practical advice and personal memoir will give hope to many readers who have known the heartache of losing their loved ones."
        —JANA RIESS, author of *The Twible* and *Flunking Sainthood*

"In *Pilgrimage through Loss*, Linda Lawrence Hunt takes us on a beautifully written and abiding journey through the evolving experiences of grief for parents after the loss of a child. Her perspectives, shared with the stories and wisdom of many other parents she interviewed, have greatly deepened my own understanding of grief. Like no stories I have heard or ever read before, she helped me see the powerful potential of the wellspring of love under a broken heart that can help in one's healing in sorrow. Through the pathways, she shares many of the ways she, her husband, and others have found to nurture this wellspring, sometimes intentionally, sometimes through other's kind friendship, and sometimes through sheer grace. This book is a most valuable resource not only to parents and their friends and family but also to physicians, therapists, and other clinicians who may accompany those who suffer such tragic losses."
        —JAMES SHAW, MD, Former Medical Director for Providence
            Center for Faith and Healing, and Palliative Care Services,
    Providence Sacred Heart Medical Center and Children's Hospital

"*Pilgrimage through Loss* doesn't tell us what we need to do but offers a gentle, wise, empathetic companion for the lonely, terrible, and grace-filled long journey of grief. As Linda Hunt grieves the loss of her loving daughter Krista and shares the stories of other parents, she articulates most profoundly and beautifully that grief is as individual and unique an experience as is the life being grieved. There are many kinds of grief and no easy answers. But there is considerable power in being reminded we are not alone, and *Pilgrimage through Loss* offers that assurance. It is a book I will reread and recommend often."

—REV. JOHN OWEN, Chaplain, U.S. Navy

"The bond between parent and child is one that endures far beyond the grave. *Pilgrimage through Loss* is not only a book about grief but also a book about love—the never-ending, boundless love of a mother's heart. The depth and breadth of Linda Lawrence Hunt's love, and thus grief, for her daughter Krista is apparent in every word, on every page, in every story, and in each glimpse of the other parent's life stories told of so many beautiful children gone too soon."

—JOANNE CACCIATORE, PhD, Founder, MISS Foundation International, and Director, Graduate Certificate in Trauma and Bereavement Program at Arizona State University

"*Pilgrimage through Loss* is like a guidebook through grief. I know many members in our congregation who are suffering from great loss, but I've not known before what they are feeling and going through. Linda Lawrence Hunt acknowledges the long journey of a parent's grief with eyes wide open to the unexpected places this journey can lead. The book is filled with compelling stories by parents on what is helpful and not-so-helpful along the way. A must-read for pastors, counselors, anyone who comes alongside those who suffer loss!"

—REV. BETSEY MOE, Associate Pastor, Hamblen Park Presbyterian Church, Spokane, Washington

"Award-winning author Linda Lawrence Hunt does it again. First, with *Bold Spirit*, now with *Pilgrimage through Loss*, she invites her readers into a soul journey of grief, compassion, and renewal. Hunt draws upon multiple stories, but it is ultimately her and Jim's story of dealing with the death of a remarkable daughter that will reach out to all of us who have experienced loss. With due respect to many books about grief, it is Hunt's spiritual insight and compelling prose that will make one reader want to tell another and another about this extraordinary book."

—RONALD C. WHITE JR., Author, *A. Lincoln: A Biography,* and Fellow, The Huntington Library

"A wonderful memoir! It took me a long time to read because I was so busy taking notes of phrases, thoughts, insights that I found fresh, creative, joyful, poignant, and memorable. It strikes a careful and appropriate balance between personal story and theological, spiritual questions. With the weaving of parents' stories throughout and the book discussion guide, this will be an excellent resource for grief groups, too."

—REV. MARILYN H. CORVIN, Retired United Church of Christ Minister, Former Staff Chaplain, Lucile Packard Children's Hospital, Palo Alto, California

"Linda L. Hunt's sensitively written book speaks profoundly to the hardest passages of human loss, but she leads the reader through such depths to a new and unexpected place. With an honesty that is both wise and unflinching, she shows us how joy does not supplant but rather transforms grieving."

—DARRELL L. GUDER, H. W. Luce Professor of Missional and Ecumenical Theology, Princeton Theological Seminary

"Thank goodness for Linda Lawrence Hunt. Her stewardship of grief, dealing with the death of her daughter, brings us *Pilgrimage through Loss*, and I am very grateful. This beautifully written and comforting book unveils with grace the paths taken by parents as they faced a great loss, the death of their child. It's not a how-to book, but it tenderly explores the many ways parents are changed by their suffering and in turn have changed others. It's also a book for aunts, uncles, grandparents, and friends who seek words and ways to offer encouragement as they walk beside those traveling through grief. Having been there, let me add: this is a book I will give to many and reread often."

—JANE KIRKPATRICK, Speaker and Author of *A Simple Gift of Comfort* and *The Daughter's Walk*

"From the first paragraph Linda Lawrence Hunt's riveting account of scorching loss cemented with my own soul. As Linda and Jim review their labyrinthine journey into the devastating loss of their daughter Krista, gentle paths from God's mercy appear. Wherever someone may have experienced profound loss in the relational self, this elegantly told account will touch and help in a deep way. I will be recommending it forever."

—Rev. Woody Garvin, Senior Minister,
Valley Presbyterian Church, Paradise Valley, Arizona

"Linda Hunt speaks to the heart of military families! Every military chaplain longs for resources like *Pilgrimage through Loss*, and Linda has given birth from her own pain and faith. It will bring much-needed aid and comfort to thousands of gold-star parents for years to come."

—Colonel Les Hyder, Retired Chaplain and Former
Director of the Air National Guard Chaplain Corps

"Linda Lawrence Hunt beautifully weaves a very personal story that could only be told many years after the death of her daughter Krista. Even amid the sorrow and anger, and then forgiveness and healing, Linda brings a message of hope and inspiration to readers. Linda shows how our hearts can expand to fully integrate this loss into our lives and encourages all who must deal with this kind of tragedy."

—Carolyn Ringo, RN, MSW, Perinatal/Pediatric
Palliative Care Coordinator, Providence Sacred
Heart Children's Hospital, Spokane, Washington

Pilgrimage through Loss

Also by the Author

Bold Spirit: Helga Estby's Forgotten Walk across Victorian America

In the Long Run: A Study of Faculty in Three Writing-across-the-Curriculum Programs

Rare Beasts, Unique Adventures: Reflections for College Students

Loaves and Fishes: A "Love Your Neighbor" Cookbook for Children

Celebrate the Seasons: A "Love Your Neighbor" Gardening Book for Children

Christina's World

Pilgrimage through Loss

Pathways to Strength and Renewal
after the Death of a Child

LINDA LAWRENCE HUNT

WESTMINSTER
JOHN KNOX PRESS
LOUISVILLE · KENTUCKY

First edition
Published by Westminster John Knox Press
Louisville, Kentucky

14 15 16 17 18 19 20 21 22 23 — 10 9 8 7 6 5 4 3 2 1

Interior design by Erika Lundbom
Cover design by Dilu Nicholas

Library of Congress Cataloging-in-Publication Data
Hunt, Linda, 1940-
  Pilgrimage through loss : pathways to strength and renewal after the death of a child / Linda Lawrence Hunt. —First edition.
    pages cm
  ISBN 978-0-664-23948-0 (alk. paper)
  1. Children—Death—Religious aspects—Christianity. 2. Grief—Religious aspects—Christianity. 3. Bereavement—Religious aspects—Christianity. I. Title.
  BV4907.H78 2014
  248.8'66--dc23
                                                                    2013041174

Most Westminster John Knox Press books are available at special quantity discounts when purchased in bulk by corporations, organizations, and special-interest groups. For more information, please e-mail SpecialSales@wjkbooks.com.

To Jim
For his vibrant daily love in times of joy and sorrow

And our families

Susan, Peter, Hunter, and Quinlen

Jefferson, Kris, and Erin

Aaron, Gabriela, Thiago, and Ava

who keep us grounded in the

joy of each day and hope-filled for the future

"Passing through the valley of Weeping, they make it a place of springs."

—Psalm 84:6 ASV

CONTENTS

PROLOGUE

NOTHING COULD HAVE PREPARED MY HUSBAND, JIM, AND ME FOR the sorrow that rocked our lives when Krista, our twenty-five-year-old married daughter, died in Bolivia. Only shrouded memories remain of the shock and grief that occurred that May 20 dawn in 1998 when we first learned that she and her husband, Aaron, were riding in a bus that plunged over a mountain cliff.

One startling memory stays vivid. The warm spring sunlight that infused our Spokane, Washington, living room suddenly shifted when storm clouds gathered later that afternoon. "Linda, come quick," Jim called. Out the French door windows, a menacing thunderstorm arced with a vibrant rainbow. A crash of thunder rumbled as he said, "Look, lightning pierced the rainbow." This fleeting sky scene gave a hint to the months and years ahead as we lived with loss that parents know pierces the soul.

Parents experience almost inconsolable grief when death takes a family's child. Whether their child is stillborn, a three-year-old, a twenty-year-old, or a forty-three-year-old, it doesn't matter. Such loss permeates with a sorrow beyond all our previous imagination. This journey into unfamiliar emotional territory turns upside down every assumption we've made in the natural order of life. The vulnerable desolation of the heart often spirals families into an abyss of emotional longing, brokenness, and pain that is hard to conceive will ever ease. Such a grief response is universal, transcending all cultures and time.

For years, a dominant theory around grief centered on the "five stages" a bereaved person goes through, from denial, anger, bargaining, and depression to acceptance. Dr. Elisabeth Kübler-Ross introduced these ideas in her 1967 book *On Death and Dying*.[1]

These became further popularized with Scribner's focused publication of Kübler-Ross's thoughts in *On Grief and Grieving: Finding the Meaning of Grief through the Five Stages of Loss* in 2005.[2] Even she said later that people didn't necessarily grieve in this "order" or experience all stages. "The trouble is that this theory turns out largely to be a fiction," claims Meghan O'Rourke in a 2010 article called "Good Grief" published in the *New Yorker*. "New research suggests that grief and mourning doesn't follow a checklist; they're complicated and untidy processes, less like a progression of stages and more like an ongoing process—sometimes one that never fully ends. . . . It's the messiness of grief that makes us uncomfortable."[3] This definitely rang more true to my own experiences.

After Krista's death, I read extensively on grief, but most books proved primarily useful in describing the early depth of disorientation and loss. Although helpful in reassuring us that our sense of devastation was normal, as the months of grief continued, I sought to understand more. Many questions surged to the surface during ensuing years; other parents echoed this reality. *Will I always feel this bad or will it be possible to savor life again? How can I keep a broken heart open? Why do I long to be alone sometimes, and other times need the comfort of friends and family? Are there ways to remember one's child that are life-affirming? Why do most men and women grieve so differently? How does one reconcile trust in a loving and powerful God with unanswered prayers for protection? Can one face grief in creative and intentional ways?* A movable feast of questions became guides in living this unchosen journey.

This caused me to wonder, *will accessing the wellspring of love that lies beneath all sorrow offer a dynamic resource for healing?*

So I began talking with other parents who had lost children. They added their voices into the silence, which often surrounds suffering. We need immense strength and even creativity to survive such loss, two qualities parents often lack during profound times of grief. They openly shared what they have learned and the creative gestures they found that eased their way. Their stories richly describe their tensions and choices while walking in the maelstrom of grief. But to these parents' astonishment, many also slowly discovered the healing energy in the reservoir of love that underlies all great loss. This caused me to wonder. *Will accessing the wellspring of love that lies beneath all sorrow offer a dynamic resource for healing?*

Such deaths ask us to expand our hearts so that we can still engage life with meaning and hope. Yet, our first temptation or need can be to shut down and close off the world. I recall at Krista's memorial service talking with a young college woman, a family friend for years. Her family had endured the horrific murder of her delightful two-year-old nephew Devon. "Molly, how have you and your family survived such a loss?" I asked. I'll never forget her response. She paused for a moment, and then said simply, "Your joys become more intense." She gave me the first inkling of what the poet Kahlil Gibran wrote in his book *The Prophet*. His poem "On Joy and Sorrow" explores how these two are inseparable. He writes, "The deeper that sorrow carves into your being, the more joy you can contain."[4] But on this day of our daughter's memorial, these words held only abstract meaning.

I think there's even more to grieving than this inseparable quality of joy and sorrow that Gibran affirms. Our family discovered, as many of these parents' stories illustrate, how our love for a child has potential to be a resource for solace, even creativity, within our broken hearts. If we stay open to this love that once graced our daily lives, we can journey through our desolation and find inner strength. Parents even describe more empathetic and expansive living, and eventual thankfulness in remembrance. However, too often the sheer pain of losing the physical presence of one we've loved, compounded by American culture's reinforcement to "move on," keeps us from being alive to this possibility. "We live in one of the world's most 'mourning-avoidant' cultures," observes Dr. Alan Wolfelt, counselor to thousands through The Center for Loss and Life Transition. He finds this attempt to prematurely shut down or repress grief hinders genuine healing.[5]

During the past fifteen years, I've learned more about ways parents access this reservoir of love, both in our own family's journey and in listening to others describe what they've experienced in the school of sorrow. One weekend I invited nine other mothers who had lost children to simply talk together. How had they responded after loss created such a seismic shift in their lives? What gestures contributed to their sense of healing? What choices had they made, and what were memorable gestures from family and friends?

Later, I interviewed more fathers and mothers who shared their stories with an amazing generosity of spirit. To my surprise, most welcomed any chance to talk of the child they lost.

Even if the death of a child occurred years before, once their stories began, the truth of their love and loss felt like death happened yesterday. Their trust in me didn't come because of my background as a writer, researcher, and professor. This meant little to them. Instead, they trusted me primarily because they sensed "you've been through this . . . you *know*."

Pilgrimage through Loss also shows how pivotal friends and family can be as they offer sustaining gifts of comfort and essential companionship during the ensuing years. Often this help can be wordless, more a fulfilling of the African saying "sit and cry with me." Friends comfort one another simply by their presence.

However, family and friends can unintentionally cause deeper harm, which inadvertently contributes to greater emotional isolation during grief. These stories are included too, such as parent's bewilderment with society's premature insistence on "getting on with life" or "closure." Even some professional grief counselors once emphasized this.

Pilgrimage through Loss also shows how pivotal friends and family can be as they offer sustaining gifts of comfort and essential companionship during the ensuing years.

Whether the child was an infant or middle-aged, whether the relationship between the parent and child at death was warm and positive or difficult, even estranged, a depth of parental love infused each of these stories. They helped me understand why there is no word in Yiddish for a parent who loses a child because "it is unspeakable."

But speak they did, with force and fragility as their hearts revisited the early years following the shock of their child's death. Parents agreed to interviews because they knew how sustaining a friend, even if only through the companionship of a book, became for them. They hungered to talk with someone who understood their journey into unknown and unwanted territory. Some parents also described the change from acute raw anguish to a deeper acceptance. As one father expressed several years after losing his son, "I can now give thanks for his being in our lives."

Parents agreed to interviews because
they knew how sustaining a friend, even
if only through the companionship
of a book, became for them.

To "heal" means to "make whole" again, "to make whole, sound, and well." The Oxford English dictionary traces the word's origin to a similar root *haelan, hela, heelen, hal,* which is the same source as health. In my mind, it does *not* mean "moving on." This book is definitely not meant to be a *prescription* on how to survive such a loss. When someone tried to comfort a father after the death of his college daughter from cancer by assuring him "You'll get over this," he was enraged. "I don't ever want to 'get over' my daughter. I will always want my daughter in my life every day." He expressed what I feel and hear from other parents. Physical death never ends our forever love of our child.

My hope is these stories help parents and their supportive communities expand and trust in their *own* ways to live with hearts intertwined with love and loss. During profound grief I wanted to read only short sections of a book, so I've tried to include just one central idea in each chapter, some discovered solace. Certain chapters may be more relevant to your own experience than others since grief has many faces. May these stories simply spark your *own* imaginative ways to draw essential inner strength.

These parents' stories also offer insight for family, friends, and others who want to come alongside someone on this journey. A discussion guide for parents and grief support groups appears at the end of the book and includes questions to encourage conversations. *Pilgrimage through Loss* invites parents, extended family, friends, and companions into this compassionate circle of other mothers and fathers who walk this road of sorrow.

I've woven our own family narrative with the stories of many other parents, grateful for what we've found meaningful on this journey no parent chooses. During the first days after Krista's death, as we waited for her injured husband, Aaron, and her body to be flown home from Bolivia, friends and family began to gather at our home. One afternoon, Woody Garvin, the pastor from First Presbyterian church in Spokane, Washington, where we worship, dropped by. His words seemed central to our next years. "Receive the gifts," he encouraged, "however strange or imperfect. People want to do something but don't know what to do."

Pilgrimage through Loss attests to the wonder of the gifts offered to those in grief. Love never dies, but our hours and days now demand a new willingness for spirited heart work to be empowered by this love. Our choices, imaginative gestures, and the power of openness can lead our broken hearts to expanded living, healing, and wholeness.

Chapter 1

ATTENDING TO A BROKEN HEART

"How could I ever prepare for an absence the size of you?"
—Mark Doty, "Coastal Home," *Heaven's Coast: A Memoir*

⚮

QUESTION: WHY IS IT IMPORTANT TO TRY TO KEEP A BROKEN
HEART OPEN AND CONSCIOUSLY ATTEND TO PROFOUND GRIEF?

When the sun rose over Mt. Spokane with the shimmering promise of a glorious May day in 1998, two couples awoke us at 6 a.m. with a knock on our door. Friends for years, they bore a message of immense sorrow. "Krista's been killed," said Ron Frase, his voice cracking with pain. "All we know so far is that a speeding bus plunged over a mountain cliff in Bolivia. We understand Aaron is injured, but alive." Both couples, colleagues of ours at Whitworth University, had known Krista since she was an endearing, spritely one-year-old, and loved her like family. Shortly before Krista and her husband, Aaron, left for a three-year volunteer assignment in Bolivia, these same friends joined at a gathering in our home to offer blessings and prayers for their upcoming service adventure. We also prayed for their safety.

After initial training in Santa Cruz, Bolivia, Krista and Aaron worked alongside indigenous Quechua families in Bañado de la Cruz, a remote river valley 7,000 miles from our home in Spokane, Washington. They carried a deep hope. Living and serving within a grassroots community in a developing nation offered essential insights before attending graduate school in international development or public policy. "How can we wisely shape U.S. foreign policy in the United States if we haven't a better understanding of the implications in others' lives?" they reasoned.

Late one night, six months after their arrival, Krista and Aaron traveled from Bañado to Santa Cruz for a retreat with other volunteers in the agency that sponsored their service. One minute they slept contentedly with their puppy, Choclo, on their lap. In the next terror-filled moments, the bus careened down a mountainside, tossing Aaron and Choclo at the top of a ravine, injured but alive. Krista was thrown out hundreds of feet below. Then the bus landed precariously on its side above her body. In pitch black, with only the night stars to light the sky, Aaron scrambled down the mountainside. Pulling aside tall brush with his injured shoulder, he knelt to touch broken bodies in desperation to recognize his wife.

The Bolivian representative only knew sketchy details when he called our friends. He wanted them to break this devastating truth to us in person. As any parent who has lost a child knows, this news shattered our hearts in as many shards as the broken glass littering the mountain crevasse.

From the moment of hearing of Krista's death, friends and family came alongside to offer their comforting presence and practical help. Throughout the day, continuing phone calls from Bolivia brought new information. We learned more about the overnight hours it took to recover her from the deep ravine, and the insistence from authorities that Aaron leave his wife to go to the hospital for his injuries. Our anguish intermingled with deep concern for her young husband who had also recently lost his mother, Linda, to breast cancer.

At first, they requested us to travel to Bolivia for her burial. "Her body probably can't be flown back to America," we were advised. "It's a policy since drug smugglers often use caskets as carriers."

"What are they thinking?" I cried, frantic over this possibility. "We can't leave her sister, brother, elderly grandmother, and her friends alone here in their grief—she didn't die in a family vacuum." Hours later, we learned this dilemma had been resolved.

Susan, Krista's twenty-eight-year-old sister, planned to be married exactly one month later. Invitations had already been sent for their festive June 20 wedding in Rhode Island. When we called, her first words were, "Should I call off the wedding, Mom? How can I get married if my sister is dead?" She planned for Krista to be her maid-of-honor, expecting her to fly up shortly with Aaron for their celebration. "Let's wait a bit until you get here to decide," we suggested. "Our family might need a point of joy."

When Krista was three, we adopted Jefferson Kim, a four-year-old from Korea. So close in age, they shared plenty of the typical sibling tussles growing up. Yet we knew he cherished his little sister more than almost anyone in his life. We were unable to contact him directly on a remote island in Bristol Bay where he worked in the Alaska fishing industry, so he had to learn of his sister's death from a personnel supervisor. An added heartbreak. My mother, widowed just four months earlier, lived alone now after a sixty-year marriage. She knew intimately the grief of losing a child when my older brother, Larry, my only sibling, died at twenty-three. She rarely talked about this loss, but I knew she grieved deeply for years.

One cannot always choose the experiences
life gives, but we do have the power to
"choose one's attitude, to choose one's
way in any given circumstances."
—*Victor Frankl*

At this time, I was an English professor at Whitworth University, a liberal arts private college. I was also relishing remission from an aggressive breast cancer a few years earlier. Besides teaching writing classes, I team-taught with four other faculty in a Western Civilization core course. A pivotal concept that helped me through cancer came from one of the books we read, Victor Frankl's *Man's Search for Meaning*. An Austrian psychiatrist, the author barely survived the Holocaust after years in horrific concentration camps, including Auschwitz. Astutely observant, he became interested in the interior lives of individuals when he discovered that some prisoners could transcend the terror and daily evil of their existence. They lived with eloquent courage, compassion, and dignity, even offering comfort and giving away their last scrap of bread to others.

Convinced that "human choice" made the pivotal difference in survival, Frankl calls this response "the last of human freedoms" after everything is taken away. One cannot always choose the experiences life gives, but we do have the power to "choose one's attitude, to choose one's way in any given circumstances."[1] His insights shaped my response to cancer, especially the harsh chemotherapy treatments, keeping me grateful for the gifts of modern medicine and deep friendships.

He considered this power to choose our attitude a vestige of spiritual freedom. Frankl found himself pondering the Russian author's Dostoevsky's wish, "There is only one thing I dread: not to be worthy of my sufferings."[2] Frankl became convinced that "if there was meaning in life at all, then there must be a meaning in suffering." He also observed that believing in a hope and a future, especially personal goals, sometimes even kept prisoners alive. Those who shut down in hopelessness often died within days. Their inner life became the powerful determinate of their future.

I had been steeped theoretically in Frankl's ideas each semester for several years and valued students' engagement with his insights. But it became even more personal when Jerry Sittser, a close friend and one of our faculty team members, suffered a catastrophic loss. In one night in 1991, a drunk driver killed three generations of women in his family. His wife, daughter, and mother died in a car accident after attending a Pow Wow for their home-schooled children on a Native American reservation. Through the bleak months and years following this, I was invited into this friend's profound journey of loss, often over a cup of coffee or during a walk on campus. He began pondering how all people suffer loss of various degrees and their varying responses. He also joined in asking Frankl's questions, such as, "How can we grow through suffering? How can one absorb suffering into one's life, rather than live with any illusion you'll get over it?" Before Krista died, I'd read early drafts of his reflections on these questions, which ultimately emerged in his thought-provoking book *A Grace Disguised: How the Soul Grows through Loss.*[3]

I vividly remembered a conversation Jerry and I shared one morning. After visiting the funeral home and staring at the coffins of his wife, daughter, and mother, he entered weeks of unimaginable anguish that he likens to existential darkness. Walking across campus together before class, he said, "After a terrifying dream last night, I had an amazing conversation with my sister. I dreamed of elusively chasing the setting sun, running west, wanting desperately to remain in its fiery warmth and light." In his dream, he collapsed in despair when he looked east at the vast darkness closing in on him. "I thought at that moment I would live in darkness forever." But his sister reminded him that *the shortest distance to the light of the sun is to go east through the darkness until one comes to the sunrise.*

This became an important truth for Jerry, recognizing there was no way to flee from his pain. "I recognized at this moment that darkness was inevitable and unavoidable, and to face the loss the best I could, rather than flee from it," he told me. "I wanted to allow myself to be transformed by suffering, rather than have any illusion I could avoid it, and yield to the loss wherever this would take me."

A newer friendship that developed shortly before Krista's death also gave me a glimpse at the pain that lay ahead. Mary Beth Baker, a mother around my age, audited my Journal Writing and Autobiography night class. She needed to write through her enormous grief over the sudden death of her twenty-seven-year-old son, Stephen, in a motorcycle accident. Her poignant essays gave me a glimpse into pain so primal and love so profound, they brought you into the heart of mother-love.

These companions who laid out their raw grief gave me a compass point. Their lives demonstrated how all-encompassing grief *demands* attention. They showed me that any healthy emotional survival from such potentially debilitating loss depended partly on my own choices on how to respond. But after May 20, the day of Krista's death, it wasn't an academic exercise.

"I recognized at this moment that darkness was inevitable and unavoidable, and to face the loss the best I could, rather than flee from it."
—Jerry Sittser

During the early days, as we waited for Aaron's return and for Krista's body to arrive from Bolivia, I thought a lot about the sudden death of my brother, Larry, in a car accident. Almost the same age as Krista; it seemed too similar to believe.

One afternoon, longing for a few moments of solitude, I slipped out to the front porch to sort out some of the thoughts and feelings swirling inside me. Part of my bewilderment was that there was no way on earth the death of such a luminous young woman made sense. Krista was beloved by her husband, her family, her students, and friends, and wanted to use her education and talents in service to others. Like that of my brother Larry, her hope and beauty and springs of joy came from her quiet confidence in a loving Creator. Whether providing leadership as the student-body president in a large high school; studying biology, government, and women's studies in college; starting a peer-tutoring program for inner-city high school students while teaching in Tacoma; or cooking alongside Quechua women on her Bañado front porch, she entered life with zest, creativity, and compassion. With her unfathomable death, it felt like not just our family lost, but the world lost too. *Where was God's protective hand?*

Probably because of enduring my brother's death earlier, I sensed that trying to "understand" this loss would be impossible. I'd lived long enough to recognize that all people in life experience suffering. It's inevitable. Years of reading student essays showed me that even by the late teens, many had already suffered loss over the death of siblings and parents, broken homes, serious health crisis, sexual abuse, or domestic violence. Even a parent's unemployment or the destructive impact of poverty shaped their lives. Though I had no illusion that anything can keep us from experiencing such losses, my core belief was that God absolutely promises to be alongside us in these times of trouble. So in a quiet, candid prayer, I said, *Krista's death seems senseless, but I will try to keep my heart as open as possible, and not shut down.* I wanted, somehow, in spite of what I may *feel*, to trust in God's presence and believe in the biblical assurance in the twenty-third Psalm (KJV), "Even though I walk through the shadow of death . . . thou art with me." Despite pain, I didn't want to lose trust in life itself.

So in a quiet, candid prayer, I said, *Krista's death seems senseless, but I will try to keep my heart as open as possible, and not shut down.*

Like the warming blankets that nurses now place on patients before hospital surgery, I was most likely insulated by emotional shock during these early days. In the months and years that followed, when little could ease the suffering that wrenched my heart, this choice to stay open and trusting was severely tested. I explained to a friend, "Maybe it's because I carried Krista in my womb, but it feels like I've just been ripped apart." Other parents talk of a "hole" and "incompleteness" and "utter emptiness." Two mothers who met almost ten years after the death of their sons and wrote *A Broken Heart Still Beats* expressed how lingering grief can be. "When Mary and I met, we had two things in common: we had lost our sons and we had lost our way. Over and over we'd wandered the trails of sadness, anger and guilt, hoping to come upon a new vista or fork that would lead us . . . who knows where, but somewhere different."[4]

Another mother, Sarah Bain, expressed this enduring nature of loss seven years after giving birth to a stillborn daughter. Born in the springtime, they named the child they held for only four hours, Grace. Sarah still physically feels deep sadness. "Every May my body just seems to go crazy and I have a kind of emotional franticness for weeks. Then I remember why."

Another factor shaped my decision to try to stay open. Because I had recently completed extensive chemotherapy for breast cancer, medical friends expressed concerns. "Beware of bottling up your pain because burying stress inside could be very unhealthy, even dangerous for you." I knew they spoke with wisdom and love, another compelling reason to keep my heart open amid grief.

Grief therapists concur. As psychiatrist Mark Epstein wrote in a *New York Times* 2013 article, "The closest one can find to a consensus about grief among today's therapists is the conviction that the healthiest way to deal with trauma is to lean into it, rather than keep it at bay."[5]

One of the gifts that came during cancer was a friendship that developed with Karlene Arguinchona. I met her when I landed in the hospital after a severe reaction to Neupogena medicine, typically used to elevate very low blood counts caused by chemotherapy. An emergency room doctor, she regularly comes close to families facing catastrophic loss. Seeing the shock of parents losing a child led her to begin a mothers' support group in her home that met once a month. Some were experiencing a recent tragedy; for others it had been years ago. "A child's life is forever important and parents need a safe place to talk about the child they've lost . . . even years later," she believes.

Karlene likens deep grief to an acute laceration that inevitably leaves a scar. She explains to mothers, "When we suture a severe injury and patients are worried about the potential for scarring, we try to help them *see how much their own efforts and attention to the care of the wound makes a difference.* For a certain period of time, the scar is more vulnerable." She then explains the active role that patients must make in their healing. "The wound needs to be kept clean and dry, out of the sun, and protected from high impact bumps. *The skin wants to heal, but it's essential that the deep wound heals on the inside as well.*" She then adds that the scar will change each day, week, and months—even years later. "A lot depends on how one takes care of it. For example, with too much sun exposure, some persons will hyper-pigment, or a high impact bump can be damaging." But she also wants patients to understand that *no matter what, there will always be a scar.* She believes grief is like this.

Even after these encounters with wise friends who made clear the choice one must make to "attend" to grief, I had no idea of the depth and length of sorrow, the scarring, and vulnerability that lay ahead. Just to get up in the morning and function in daily responsibilities sometimes proved daunting, let alone to make specific efforts to take care of this deep wound that any bereaved parent feels. I think poet Mark Doty expressed the loss that lay ahead best with his words, "How could I ever prepare for an absence the size of you?" Krista's "permeating presence of absence" loomed everywhere.

Chapter 2

FINDING SOLACE
IN SHARED STORIES

"The most terrifying human disease is denial."

—Words from a bereaved father after a lifelong friend visited
and never once mentioned the loss of his daughter.

⚶

QUESTION: WHAT ARE CREATIVE WAYS TO SHARE STORIES
THAT WILL PROVIDE SOLACE?

Wen a loved one dies, one of the most common early reactions is an intense yearning, a sense that a part of you is missing, and a hunger to have them come back. This news actually surprised grief researchers at Yale University and the Dana Farber Center, who expected depression to be the dominant emotion after a death. In sharing stories about a loved one who has died, such reminiscences often help ease the yearning and heartbreak.

However, to the dismay of many bereaved parents, after a brief time many people rarely want to talk about the dead child in fear this will be too upsetting. These silences add another layer of pain. "Ours was a family bound by an unacknowledged credo," says Solveig Torvik in the introduction to *Nikolai's Fortune*, a family memoir she wrote to unearth four generations of Norwegian silences. "They tended to believe that if a thing remains unspoken, it does not exist; if pain is given no voice, it lacks power to harm."[1] Many war veterans I once taught at a community college also admitted they carried their pain in silence in vain hopes it might go away.

These silences add another layer of pain.
"Ours was a family bound by an unacknowledged credo. . . . They tended to believe that if a thing remains unspoken, it does not exist; if pain is given no voice, it lacks power to harm."
—*Solveig Torvik*

One father told of longtime friends who came from another state to visit a year after the death of his adult daughter. "Our children grew up together, so I was really looking forward to this reunion with friends who knew my daughter. I was eager to share memories. But they were here for three days and the wife never *once* mentioned my daughter or her death," he said to me, still clearly astonished and hurt by her choice. "Her husband put his arm around me while we were in the garage and said simply, 'I can't imagine what it must feel like to give up a child, but I'm so sorry this ever happened.' That was all I needed to hear." He just shook his head and added, "The most terrifying human disease is denial."

Often memorial services open the door for others to share stories that speak to our yearning. Hundreds joined us at a service for Krista on May 26, 1998, which happened to be the third anniversary of her wedding. Sitting beside Aaron in the same First Presbyterian sanctuary where they once exchanged marriage vows gave new poignancy to the promise "until death do us part." It seemed unfathomable that where she once stood as a radiant bride, we now saw her beautiful physical presence reduced to ashes in a Shaker box.

I was surprised to see Moses Pulei. A Masai tribal leader from Kenya, he flew up from his seminary studies in California. I remember the day he entered my writing class at Whitworth University, just hours after he arrived from Nairobi. A former World Vision sponsored child, and grandson of a respected village elder known as one of the "holy people," Moses was among the first to benefit when the government insisted Masai children be educated. His intelligence and facility with languages, plus his natural leadership skills, led to his entrance into an American college.

He met Krista one Easter brunch at our home, but that was all we knew. In the reception line afterward, he asked, "Could I come to visit you in your home? In the Masai tradition, when someone dies, the greatest gift we can give is to go to the family's home and share a story."

Later that week he told us a story we'd never heard. "Shortly after coming to Spokane, I went downtown with another African student. While walking on the street, a group of men drove by in a pickup, threatening us. They called us 'niggers' and 'monkeys,' and yelled at us to 'go back to Africa.'" He'd never experienced such direct aggressive racism because of the color of his skin. "I was frightened and angry, and just wanted to go back home to Kenya. I had a return ticket and planned to use it."

Back on campus, he told his student host about his fears. For some reason, his friend, who studied with Krista in Central America earlier, told Moses, "You've got to meet Krista Hunt." Although she attended the University of Puget Sound in Tacoma, she happened to be in Spokane visiting. "What she said changed my life," he told us. After describing to Krista what happened and his desire to return home, she encouraged him not to make a hasty decision. "Moses, when this happens again," she said, "you *have* to remember that the problem is not in you, but in the persons treating you this way." Then she added, "If you let these men deter you from your goals, you'll never achieve what you came to America to do. You want to be in control of your life decisions, not let them determine your future."

He took her words to heart. Rather than shut down with fear, he decided to stay in America and be his warm, sociable Kenyan self. He became so beloved among students that they elected him as their first international student-body president. His brilliance and commitment as a scholar led to graduate scholarships while earning his PhD. He continued to go back and forth between Kenya and America, representing the Masai in government negotiations, aiding in drought relief, and connecting Americans and Kenyans in common projects, such as an orphanage and a high school for girls. "Without Krista's encouragement, I often wonder how different my life would be."

This was only the beginning of the many friends who gave us further glimpses of Krista's life. Sometimes we learned of previously held secrets. Her sister, Susan, told us of the time when she and Krista won a national cooking contest and a trip to New York City. The college "chaperone" took the teenage sisters to a popular café where they were served alcohol. Although only fourteen-years old, at 5'10" and fashionably dressed, she relished passing for twenty-one. Her college friends revealed new stories of adventures, experimentation, and humorous escapades of life on campus. Several friends sent copies of her delightful and reflective e-mails from Bolivia. When a parent loses a child, each additional story gives a part of the person back. It is undoubtedly one of the finest gifts that a caring friend or relative can give.

Six years after Krista died, I invited a group of mothers to an October weekend retreat to share their stories. Each lost her child in different ways, whether through a prolonged illness or sudden death, and at different ages. Also the nature of the relationship they enjoyed with their child differed. But one thing they all agreed on was "we just long to hear someone say our child's name." "When we go to family reunions," said one mother whose son died a few years earlier, "no one wants to mention our son. I know it is because they are afraid it will make us sad and I'll cry. But it's like he's erased from family memory."

> But one thing they [mothers] all
> agreed on was, "we just long to hear
> someone say our child's name."

Because a shroud of silence so often emerges, some parents found it helpful to signal to friends of their need to still talk about their child. Babs Egolf, upset that within weeks her friends never mentioned her sixteen-year-old son again, invited thirty people to join her family for another memorial time when they spread her son's ashes at South Baldy Mountain. "I primarily invited them so I could tell them, 'please talk with me about my son. Don't be afraid. I need to keep Wade alive in my memory.'" Once her friends understood that she wanted this, they felt comfortable bringing him up in conversation.

But very often, friends and family find a mosaic of tangible ways to help parents keep memories alive. Whether in scrapbooks, photograph displays, quilts made of favorite fabrics, an annual birthday dinner that includes cherished memories and foods, or a DVD with favorite songs, these stories ease the soul. "I'm comforted every day by the quilt my friend Dawn helped make of my son's t-shirts," says Sheree Capulli after her son died in a car accident. "Each shirt brings good memories of different times in his life."

When Mary Beth and Dick Baker lost their only son, Stephen, a strapping 6'5" marine biologist and singer, a lifelong friend sent them a notebook of letters he wrote to her. He'd been working on a very difficult assignment as a government Fishery Observer for the National Oceanic and Atmospheric Administration (NOAA) on the *Ocean Prowler*, a 155-foot long fishing vessel in the Bering Sea. Bekah and Stephen shared their love of music, nature, art, travel, and faith quest since childhood days. Killed by a truck in a motorcycle accident on the Seattle freeway, these letters gave his parents intimate insight into his life as a twenty-seven-year-old male on the threshold of life's major decisions. Two weeks after setting sail, he writes:

Dear Bekah,

2320 hours and all is quiet aboard the Sea Quail. We are anchored up in a protected harbor of N.E. Kodiak Island and have shut down for the night. This is the first privacy that I have felt since coming aboard . . . it is very lonely at times. That is when I think of home, people, and places left behind. God strengthens me at these times, making His presence known in small ways: the lapping of the water on the boat, the twilight of stars at midnight, or the afternoon flock of sea gulls tempting you to reach out and touch their wings. All these things God made, and they bring me joy. It is amazing how all of the little things make all the difference.

"He'd been away to college, Europe, and jobs, so he'd grown a lot as a young man," recalls his dad. "I felt like these letters gave us a glimpse of the man he was becoming." They bound these letters into a collection "Letters from a Bering Sea" for the family; they also donated a copy for the Clearwater Lodge conference guest room named in Stephen's honor. Now others who visit the Presbyterian camp he loved as a child and teenager share in his memory.

Another mother, Carol Koller, also spoke of how much it meant to hear stories even years after her daughter Heather's death. One of Krista's most significant friends, Heather was a neighbor child she met at age three. They bonded deeply during the next eighteen years as Heather battled four bouts of cancer beginning when she was only six. Her initial treatments of chemotherapy lasted two long years. Her oncology doctor said, "one day we will look back on how we treated these kids as the dark ages of medicine."

"Courage is going close to
where you don't want to be."
—*A child facing harsh chemotherapy treatments*

"Krista was sunshine on two legs," Carol recalled as she spoke at Krista's memorial service. She then told of how the family invited Krista over when six-year-old Heather needed to endure another daunting chemotherapy treatment. "Heather would be refusing to get out of bed, but within minutes after Krista arrived, I'd hear the girls giggling in the bedroom, playing with Yankee, our irrepressible black Lab. Pretty soon she could get up to face one more hospital visit." In these days, chemotherapy needles dripped directly into a child's veins, prior to the invention of port implantations. "It could be brutal," remembers Carol. Another child in the hospital gave Carol an insightful definition of courage when he also entered harsh treatments. "Courage is going close to where you don't want to be."

We knew that Heather taught Krista lifelong lessons about courage as they traveled this journey together. Whether tackling bicycle mountain climbs at cancer camp, figuring out fashionable junior-high ways to wear a wig, or learning to let go of impossible dreams as Heather's once flexible ballet body lost strength, Krista grew from knowing Heather. She learned early about the fragility of life, internal strength, and the importance of treasuring each day.

Shortly after Heather's graduation from Pacific Lutheran University, where students selected her to be their Scandinavian Lucia Bride, she endured her fourth and fatal cancer. Shortly before she died, she told her mother, "Mom, I will come to you when you least expect me."

Almost eight years later, a box came in the mail. On the outside it said, "If you are the parents of Heather Koller, this is for you. If not, please return." "Because of what Heather had said to us, I was filled with joyful anticipation," said Carol. "We had moved into a new town where no one knew Heather growing up, so for someone to acknowledge her was so rare." Inside the box rested a glass kitchen jar with a cork and narrow pink, white, and magenta ribbons around the neck. Pieces of fold-over paper filled the inside. With it came a card that said:

> I was a girl in junior-high that Heather befriended. I was not part of the popular group and I was making very bad choices that weren't good for me. Heather gave this jar to me to help me get through some very difficult times. I've made it, am happily married with two beautiful girls, and now I think it belongs to you.

Carol remembers being stunned. "Heather had never said a word to anyone about doing this. It was just a quiet gesture of love for this person. I took the lid off and realized that every piece of paper had been handwritten by Heather. I felt like I could just see her sitting at her desk carefully making each one." Carol read a few of them, but then stopped. She decided she'd rather savor these inspiring words from her daughter, one or two a day. In pink ink, probably written by Heather at age twelve or thirteen after she had been in years of cancer treatment, she wrote these encouraging words to her young friend.

> Enjoy the little things in life; for one day you might look back and discover they were the big things.

> Some say it's holding on that makes you strong; sometimes it's letting go.

> Don't be afraid to take a big step if one is indicated; you can't cross a chasm in two small jumps.

Now and then Heather included biblical verses that her mom knew encouraged her daughter's unusual strength of spirit, such as these words from the New Testament found in Philippians 4:6–7:

> Rejoice in the Lord always; I will say it again; rejoice; let your gentleness be evident to all; the Lord is near; do not be anxious about anything, but in everything, by prayer and petition, with thanksgiving, present your requests to God. (NIV)

Eventually Carol wrote these all down in a book and gave the jar and writings away when a close college friend of Heather's gave birth to a daughter and named her Heather. "I've waited so long to have a baby girl I could raise like Heather and share my love of Heather with her," she wrote. For a baby gift, Carol gave this jar of inspiration to Heather's namesake.

Obviously, sometimes the stories we hear are not so joyful, even hurtful and hard. When Steve, a thirty-eight-year-old son of friends of ours, jumped out a window after years of battling with mental illness, the family's devastation was enormous. "He appeared to be getting better, was back in college, and working hard to earn the right to restore his relationship with his two beloved daughters," said Sharon Clegg, his mother. Earlier, in the depths of his depression when he refused to take medication, he made some terrible choices. These threatened others and led to a jail sentence.

Hundreds gathered at the memorial service to support the family, including his divorced wife and their two children. His father, Doug, spoke candidly of his acute awareness that during Steve's down times, his behaviors created immense pain for some gathered in the chapel. He expressed a hope that they, like his own family who often suffered heartbreak, even dangers, from Steve's actions, could eventually forgive. Alongside this truth lived another reality as those who knew Steve intimately shared photographs and examples of his generosity, his commitment to friendship, his academic achievements, and his service in the military. Tender photographs showed his father's heart of love toward his young daughters before their estrangement. Regaining parental visitation rights motivated his desire to get well. He missed them dearly. Even the very clean and orderly apartment and inspirational books he kept reflected a side of his personality that spoke to his new efforts at regaining health. For his family, especially his two children, these stories spoken in love gave a measure of peace.

It was this permanent loss of her joyful presence that almost overwhelmed us in the early months.

Even a heartfelt note offers solace. One day a tiny card came from the cook that knew Heather and Krista from their summer days at a Presbyterian camp. She remembered their loyal friendship. It showed a large sailboat leaving shore heading off into the vast ocean. I don't recall the exact words, but the message was simply that when those on one shore say, "There she goes," others on the distant shore are excitedly saying, "Here she comes." I was touched by the cook's tender thought of Heather welcoming Krista into this mysterious afterlife through this metaphor for the Christian belief in eternity. Her gentle conviction that this life is only part of one's story echoed what gave comfort to me.

One of the greatest treasures we received came from a stranger, Jeremy Funk, who also volunteered in Bolivia. He met Krista and Aaron while they trained in Santa Cruz and struck up a special friendship, often while cooking meals together. A talented writer who struggles with the challenges of cerebral palsy, he was touched deeply by her joy of life. A memory he cherished happened when Krista insisted he dance with her at a festive Quinceañera party, the celebration for fifteen-year-old girls in Latin American countries. Unable to sleep the night he learned of her death, he wrote *Joy Dance,* a poem that we shared at her memorial and many other occasions. After celebrating her joy in several stanzas, he concludes:

If I cannot prolong your dance, I will
proclaim it. I will proclaim your dance
to God and to the world. I will celebrate
a dance of flavors: tomatoes, oregano, basil
when you cooked pasta with me in the kitchen.

I will remember how you made me laugh,
how laughter swam in your voice.
I won't forget the way you giggled and tugged
at Aaron's questions across the supper table,
both wishing for a cup of Starbucks coffee.

Paging through my journal and listening
to the night. I hear hens in
recitative. Dogs whimper,
leaves flap, or angel-wings.
Treetops bend and rock, like my spirit
this night: bowing yet dancing.
And in the breeze that lures these trees to praise
I almost hear you singing hallelujah.[2]

It was this permanent loss of her joyful presence that almost overwhelmed us in the early months. But both strangers and friends continued to give us glimpses of the texture of Krista's life. Some stories even gave us moments of laughter, a welcome relief from sorrow.

"You seem to like to talk about Krista," said Aaron and Krista's supervisor in Bolivia, a single man in his forties. "My mother died when we were young and she was never talked about in the family again. I think we're all the poorer for it," he said wistfully.

Other grieving parents expressed what we experienced, that stories shared settle in the broken heart and affirm that love will live forever. As Moses showed our family, even death doesn't have to part us from the healing power within our stories.

Chapter 3

TAKING SMALL STEPS DAILY

"A blessing. That you do not know at the moment of impact how far-reaching the shock waves will be. . . . Only a year and a half. Still, it is a long time to discover that you are still in shock, still in the infant stages of recovery."

—Judith Guest, *A Broken Heart Still Beats*

❧

QUESTION: HOW IN THE WORLD DOES ONE FUNCTION LIVING WITH SUCH ACUTE PAIN?

In the early weeks, after most friends and family returned home and all the significant decisions around her memorial services had been made, I found myself almost frozen with grief. One image that seems to describe this trauma of losing a child comes from Sharon Parks, Susan and Krista's godmother. In her book *Big Questions, Worthy Dreams*, she shares the metaphor of "shipwreck, gladness and amazement," originally created by theological-ethicist Richard Niebuhr.[1] One suffers a "shipwreck" experience when people undergo the breakup or unraveling of what has held their world together, a ripping into the fabric of life. The death of a child, the loss of a relationship through divorce or betrayal, violence, the collapse of a career . . . some suffering that collapses our sense of self, the world, and God. This resonates with one meaning of the word *bereavement* which is "to tear apart."

One suffers a "shipwreck" experience when people undergo the breakup or unraveling of what has held their world together, a ripping into the fabric of life.

Shipwreck occurs when what has dependably served as shelter and protection, holding and carrying us where we wanted to go, comes apart. What once promised trustworthiness vanishes. Our sense of "family," of "self-identity" as a parent, and our trust in the natural order of things all change when a child dies. For some, this includes earlier trust in a loving God. Whether it is young parents who lose a baby instantly to SIDS or an aging widow who loses her sixty-year-old son slowly from cancer, the loss is irretrievably a life-altering shipwreck experience. I'll never forget how, when my brother died, my father retreated to bed and refused to move for days. This left my mother and I alone to cope with all the choices and planning around his burial and memorial service. So paralyzed by grief, he almost missed his son's memorial service. It is not so just for parents, but also shapes the lives of siblings, extended family, and friends.

How in the world does one function with this kind of screaming pain, I wondered. I never wanted to leave the house, felt indecisive about almost everything, and avoided any casual contact with people. Solitude seemed essential, as welcome as fresh mountain air. Finally, Jim gently said, "Honey, you can't just lock yourself up in the house. The Art Fest is in town . . . let's just go down for a little while." He knew that I always enjoyed this juried art show. Northwest artisans display their handcrafted jewelry, heirloom toys, medieval musical instruments, and contemporary paintings and pottery, truly a feast of color and design. But it's also the kind of place where we inevitably encounter friends and acquaintances. Encounters I dreaded.

But his persuasiveness overcame my reluctance. When we arrived at the park, the aromas of Greek gyros, Asian spices, and fresh baked baklava wafted in the air. Children with painted clown faces danced to the beat of drums from a lively rock band on a nearby stage, all sights that normally lifted one's spirits. Instead, I flashed back to a memory of a friend's comments the morning her adopted baby from Korea died in the nearby city hospital. "Lori Jo died from an eye disease that could have been prevented with just a little bit of money for medicine. But, it was money the orphanage didn't have," lamented Chris Embleton. "As we left the hospital and drove home the morning after our baby died, I couldn't believe the normalcy of the world. 'Our baby is dead!' I wanted to shout. Everything in our family life was now so different. But that's one of the shocks. The world, in fact, goes on." Eventually, Chris turned her own profound bereavement and anger at such global health inequities into the founding of Healing the Children. This organization brings children with acute medical needs from around the world for treatment in American hospitals. As I looked around the Art Fest at such joyful normalcy, I finally understood what she told me years ago.

After a while, Jim saw a music booth he wanted to visit at the same moment an exquisite pottery stand drew my attention. While home with preschool children, I'd taken pottery classes at the YWCA and still loved the shapes and glazes that distinguished each potter's touch.

So many people warned us that "everything is different after you lose a child." I felt resentful, even though I suspected some truth hovered within this glib comment. Jim and I had already talked about this assertion and expressed hope that some things wouldn't change in the life we shared. One was a lifelong love of simple hospitality, opening our hillside home and sharing potluck meals with others. Though I didn't want much interaction with anyone but our closest family and friends, my hope was this aversion wouldn't endure.

When I entered the artist's booth, her cobalt blue and enchanting golden sunflower pottery exuded such a joie de vivre I couldn't help but smile. During my recent graduate studies, I discovered that early American and Norwegian feminists claimed the sunflower as a symbol of a woman's right to light and air and an optimistic spirit. I'd just written a doctoral thesis on a Norwegian immigrant mother and daughter who walked across America in 1896 on a $10,000 wager trying to save their family farm. Unable to pay their taxes and mortgage, they exemplified a mother's determination to shape their lives, not be passive victims of life circumstances. In this Victorian era, the sunflower proved a potent accessible symbol for women.

Seeing the potter's table of sunny beauty, I felt my first clarity in decision making. After weeks of muddled indecisiveness, I knew I wanted to bring home a piece as a reminder that someday we would invite others over again. The potter's high prices, well-deserved, meant I needed to choose just one. The challenge was which one. Did I want the stunning large serving plate, or an ample lidded bowl, useful for homemade soups and casseroles? While debating this, an acquaintance came by. Judy Mandeville, a young mother and creative dance instructor, loved the potter's touch too. I was surprised at how much I enjoyed our casual conversation about an artist's talents. *Maybe being in public environments again is possible*, I thought. I chose the lidded casserole, and she decided to purchase the large serving plate. After paying the artist, Judy spontaneously turned and handed me her package. "God wants me to give this to you," she said. Taken aback and startled by her generous gesture, I started to hesitate. But I knew she lived attentive to the nudging of God's spirit in her life. The sincerity in her voice reminded me of the guidance our pastor gave to "receive the gifts." So I thanked her for such extravagant kindness and left humbled with this foretaste of God's abiding grace in our sorrow. At home, I placed the bowl and the vibrant plate on the dining room buffet. This daily reminder of generosity reinforced my desire that our home might once again welcome guests and strangers.

"We must mourn, but we must go on living."
—*A widower raising three children*

Other friends shared life wisdom and comfort in the letters and cards that kept pouring in. A friend from college days included the guidance *Just Do the Next Thing,* which she heard author Elizabeth Elliot explain at a women's retreat in Colorado. Widowed twice, Elizabeth discovered these five pivotal words on a small stone church in an English village. They offered a practical way to live during the days of mourning, a way that seemed manageable. They resonated with what another friend said about the delicate tension one lives with in grief. "We must mourn, but we must go on living." In his case, this meant coming home to cook dinner and raise three grieving, motherless children after teaching classes all day. After putting them to bed, he then stayed up for hours, often listening to music. He wanted to sit with the pain and allow himself to feel this. Grief counselors speak of the value of "dosing" the pain, where a person allows oneself to give genuine attention to their feelings of loss but also continues to engage in life's "next things."

This wisdom echoes the research of Dr. Robert Maurer. He explains in his book *The Kaizen Way: One Small Step Can Change Your Life* how such attention to small efforts can ultimately be life changing. A clinical professor at the UCLA School of Medicine, he consults internationally with people and organizations, teaching the potent force of *kaizen*, the Japanese technique of achieving great and lasting success through small, steady steps. His idea is captured in the familiar saying, "A journey of a thousand miles must begin with the first step," by Lao Tzu, the Chinese philosopher considered the founder of Taoism.[2]

Grief counselors speak of the value of "dosing" the pain, where a person allows oneself to give genuine attention to their feelings of loss but also continues to engage is life's "next things."

For the next months, *Just Do the Next Thing* stayed in my mind before each hour's reality, whether it meant buying groceries and cooking supper, grading papers, paying bills, or making the decision with Susan and Peter to go ahead with their East Coast wedding. Because this involved a garden reception at our home later in the summer, the "next thing" meant we needed to plant summer flowers soon. Our neighbor, Kathleen Hume, understood my strong need for privacy so she drove me to a distant nursery where I was less likely to encounter others. She knows our garden well and selected plants she knew flourished in our short summer season, relieving my indecisiveness.

Another bereaved mother, who felt a similar hesitancy to go to grocery stores, malls, or other environments with casual interactions, mentioned how helpful it was to be forced to get up. Her "next thing" each day was to get dressed and drive her children to school. "If it wasn't for them, I doubt I would have even climbed out of bed I was in such despair."

To prepare for Susan and Peter's wedding involved more than just getting ourselves to Rhode Island. We felt genuine happiness at their commitment to one another after a four-year romance that weathered many trials and distances. We didn't want our sadness to screen out this joy. We also wanted to celebrate Susan's MBA graduation. After being with our family for her sister's memorials, she returned to take rigorous final exams. No easy task. Shortly before leaving for their wedding, Jim and I drove up to a little cabin at Priest Lake, a jewel of water in the high mountain wilderness of northern Idaho. It always served as a calming and thinking place, including where I'd made hard decisions earlier surrounding complex cancer treatment choices.

Somehow I needed to shift out of this desire to withdraw from people. I wanted to enter into a spirit of openness to the beauty of their love and to meeting Peter's family and their friends. We felt grateful that their Episcopal minister made it clear to them in marriage counseling that their wedding must not be a fourth memorial service for Krista. "It needs to be a celebration of *your* vows," he wisely insisted. He didn't want Krista's death central to the ceremony, and we didn't want our presence and grief to draw attention away from their significant commitment.

Through the years I've introduced students in my English classes to the value and craft of writing in a journal. I write episodically, but noticed that during the toughest times I tend *not* to write, the opposite of many journal writers. However, by the peaceful shore of Priest Lake, I wrote out as best as I understood, the choices around this new world of living without Krista's physical presence. I titled the journal page simply, "What I can and cannot do." Then, it just included a list.

> I will not let my feelings determine my actions
> However, I will express and trust the heart
> I can…
>> live within this deep pain and still give and receive joy
>> be a friend to Jim, Susan, Jefferson, and Aaron in their grief
>> do physical exercise to help stress
>> write "From Bolivia, with Love": Email wisdom from a young global volunteer (using Krista's emails to friends and family)
>> consciously remember to shift to gratefulness when sorrow overwhelms
>> stay interested in other's lives
>> allow myself TIME and be gentle and patient with my own grief
>> call on wonderful friends as needed.
> I cannot carry Aaron's pain, but can trust God's goodness to him and love him like a son.
> I can stay sensitive to Jim's grief and be beside him—as he is to me
> I can hope for creative ways to honor her memory
> We can avoid obsessing or "shrining" her into St. Krista— she'd laugh and be dismayed.
> We can be grateful for Susan, Peter, and Jefferson
> I can rely on God's strength perfected in our weakness
> June 8, 1998

Somehow naming these put my heart more at ease, though I rarely read these in the months ahead. But it became a kind of internal compass, and when inertia derailed me, it simplified decisions.

Two weeks after Krista's memorial services, we flew east for graduation ceremonies in New Hampshire. Susan met us at a restaurant, radiant in a blue silk dress. But it wasn't her upcoming marriage that had her glowing with an inner happiness this evening. After we toasted her completion of studies with a glass of wine, she pulled out a one-page letter and handed it to her father. "We have to keep this a secret from our classmates until it's announced tomorrow at graduation," she said. Her excitement brimmed over notice from the faculty that they'd selected her as one of their outstanding scholars. As I watched her delight in giving her professor-father such pleasurable news, I was so glad we didn't choose to miss this treasured moment. I began to wonder, *Maybe I'll miss a lot if I give in to my feelings of wanting seclusion.*

On June 20, exactly a month after Krista's death, Peter and Susan exchanged vows in the historic seventeenth-century Trinity Episcopal Church in Newport. Sharon Parks, Susan and Krista's godmother, gave a brief comment about our family's loss in the midst of her remembrances of the girls as little sisters. Peter and Susan dedicated a bouquet of lilies in Krista's honor at the altar. But apart from this, the thoughtful pastor kept the entire focus on the joy of this new union.

Maybe I'll miss a lot if I give in to my feelings of wanting seclusion.

Jim's challenge to *just do the next thing* involved giving a father-of-the-bride toast at their festive reception overlooking the distant Atlantic Ocean. He'd been scribbling notes on the airplane, wanting to honor his beloved firstborn daughter. Rising above his sorrow, he read his joy-filled blessing, concluding with these wishes:

> May your marriage be sustained by the deep waters of a place you will call home in the harbor of your contentment.
> May your marriage weave together the best threads of your west and east coast families into a tapestry of your own design.
> May your marriage be strong enough to sustain the joys of celebration and the low points of sorrow when they come your way.

May your marriage experience the presence of God who will
quicken your hearts together in compassion for others,
including the poor, the lonely, the brokenhearted, the
traveler, and the outcasts in society.

May the crowd of friends and relatives now surrounding
you become a cloud of witnesses to your sustaining
friendship and love.

June 20th 1998

Then we all lifted our glasses of champagne and Jim danced
the night away with Susan, the bridesmaids, and me, definitely
a much-needed point of joy for our family.

But for Aaron, watching most of this from the sidelines, it
meant reliving his wedding and reception with Krista just three
years earlier. Bereft, with his own dreams shattered, I couldn't
imagine the swirl of emotions he must be experiencing. But
we were so heartened by his courage to come.

Chapter 4

TRUSTING OURSELVES
IN THE MIDST OF GRIEF

*We know little, but that we must trust in what is difficult
is a certainty that will never abandon us.*

—Rainer Maria Rilke, "Letters to a Young Poet"

ca/W°

QUESTION: WILL TRUSTING OUR OWN INSTINCTS AND TIMING,
ESPECIALLY WHEN OTHERS ADVISE DIFFERENTLY, HELP EASE
OUR JOURNEY?

When encouraged to "receive the gifts," we didn't know at the time we'd be offered the gift of visiting Bolivia, the land of Krista and Aaron's last six months of life together. Then her service agency, the Mennonite Central Committee (MCC), invited us to see the country and meet the people that so captured Krista's heart.

Some family and friends questioned whether we should go. Was it really wise to embark on one more emotionally laden experience? Susan's wedding took our family on a roller coaster of immense joy and sorrow, especially for Aaron, but it added to our fatigue. Knowing we needed to travel the same dangerous roads if we visited Bolivia fueled our family's fears.

Yet we knew if we didn't accept this gift now, parts of Krista's story could be lost forever. We had lost too much already with the loss of her future. How could we bear refusing to know the last six months of her life? We longed to meet her new friends in Santa Cruz and in the village cooperative, and see the fertile Bañado de la Cruz river valley, which she wrote gave her a "peace which seeps into my soul." Aaron took a photograph the day before she died. She's preparing to climb on her Honda motorbike wearing her baseball cap askew. With their puppy Choclo's head peeking out of a cloth sling on her back, and a large pack strapped to the cycle, she looks bound for adventure. It reminded me that young adults grow significantly within a few months in a challenging environment. I didn't want to freeze-dry Krista's image in memories that left out her daily actions in global service. We knew we needed to go while fresh remnants of her memory still lived in those who had known her for only a few short months. So we chose this journey into terrible beauty.

We began this pilgrimage to the land of our daughter's last days on earth in August, three months after her death. We came because it was a gift offered and because we couldn't imagine our son-in-law going back to close up their first home without family support. As our airplane lifted off from La

Paz, the last leg of a seven-thousand-mile journey to Santa Cruz, Bolivia, Jim, Aaron, and I felt drawn to the window to view the towering Illimani Mountain. Much like on majestic Mt. Rainier that crowns our home state of Washington, ragged glacier crevasses give visual warning to the inherent dangers en route to the summit. Understandably, passengers seemed enchanted by the dazzling view. However, we were not tourists seeking a summit experience in an exotic land, but a mother and father and young husband ragged with grief as we imagined the death of our daughter and wife deep in another Andean mountain ravine. Our search was for a deeper peace to help soothe the profound shock and break in our hearts.

It still seemed incomprehensible that in one midnight moment Krista and Aaron sat wrapped in a blanket of young love in a fairly new microbus. Holding hands, they rested peacefully as their puppy, Choclo, snuggled on their laps. In the next terror-filled moment, their speeding bus plunged over a high cliff, tossing passengers out the windows like rag dolls as it careened down the edge of the mountain.

Our search was for a deeper peace
to help soothe the profound shock
and break in our hearts.

At all three of Krista's memorial services, mourners sang the famous Shaker song "It's a Gift to Be Simple." There's a stanza that goes, "And when you land in the place just right, you'll be in the valley of love and delight."

In her last letters and e-mails she wrote of her increasing contentment and delight as Aaron and she settled into their one-room home in the river valley of Bañado de la Cruz. She also expressed a joy in her soul as she began to know the fifty families farming along the river. Shortly after their arrival, she'd e-mailed her pleasure at a gathering of the women's cooperative on their front porch.

Monday afternoon was the women's group reunion. We processed their future plans and then cooked our stuffed green peppers. The cooking was beautiful if it could be such a thing. We sat around cutting onions, spices, and cooking everything on the open fire. The women shifted tasks as babies cried, or children needed attention. The dogs, pigs, and chickens were always shooed away from the food scraps despite their effectiveness at cleaning up the compost.

We wondered what it was about this remote land that felt just right to her. While we hungered to become acquainted with our daughter's life in Bolivia, Aaron left the United States haunted at returning to the land filled with overwhelming memories of his wife. He hoped to show us their daily world, and he needed to decide whether he could ever return for further service. They had completed only six months of a three-year commitment in community development through the church service organization that sends volunteers to work at the grassroots level around the world.

MCC emerged in Europe after the ravages of two world wars. The year Aaron and Krista joined in 1998, the organization sent over nine hundred volunteers to fifty countries within Europe, Asia, Africa, and Latin and South America. Like Krista, who grew up in a Presbyterian tradition, volunteers come from a variety of religious backgrounds. MCC simply asks that they embrace the Christian vision of wanting to demonstrate God's love to people in practical ways in the community. They encourage serving as a mutual giving and receiving, always learning from one another. After her initial training, Krista commented that she appreciated MCC's emphasis. They stressed that though volunteers usually join in hopes of contributing in the world, it's likely that the most lasting change will be in them. MCC's hope is that volunteers return to America as engaged and thoughtful citizens who want to live with a lifelong ethic of service and interest in the world. Though MCC covered basic expenses for housing, food, and transportation, Krista and Aaron's stipend was only sixty dollars a month for incidentals.

For the first couple of days in Santa Cruz, Aaron took us to all the places they enjoyed in Bolivia's second largest city. In the MCC compound, central headquarters for the twenty-four teams in this region, we visited their urban garden courtyard. We'd seen this on a video where they held a memorial service for Krista. Unfortunately, the sounds of screeching cars, honking horns, and cawing crows almost drowned out the Spanish words of remembrance spoken by so many of her Bolivian friends. Volunteers are not naive to the dangers inherent in working in developing countries since they often serve among people who suffer daily from poverty, conflicts, risky transportation, warfare, or natural disasters. As I looked at Krista's picture hung on MCC's office wall, I noticed it hung next to two other volunteers killed in this region.

Before leaving Santa Cruz for the eight-hour pickup truck drive to Bañado, we stopped at the outdoor market. We wanted to bring fresh flowers to the accident site that we would be passing on the route. Two volunteers, Chris and Lorie, joined us to provide comfort, directions, and essential language translations. To my amazement, I found the same rare brandy and cream roses that graced Susan's wedding. I gathered a bouquet, imagining roses from Susan, daisies from her childhood friend Julienne Gage, carnations from Jim, and added snapdragons, a favorite of Krista's childhood. Aaron selected a classic long-stemmed red rose.

Even major highways in Bolivia deteriorate to wretched roads, distressing drivers seeking to avoid sand traps, mud holes, cracked surfaces, and the swirling dust devils in the dry season. We bounced along for almost four hours through rural countryside before Lorie warned, "we're almost here." Shortly after, we rounded the corner to what newspapers called "the death curve."

Two crosses adorned with gaudy plastic flowers mark the site. Authorities had recently removed the bus and now a long swath clearing scarred the dense brush in the mountainside. It looked similar to a ski slope in Washington State's Snoqualmie Pass in the summer. Cheerful high shrubs, with sun-yellow daisy flowers gave no hint to the May 20 night of violence. Yet three persons lost their lives and dozens suffered injuries as the speeding microbus flew over a bank of trees before crashing down the mountain.

Aaron relived aloud his memories of that fateful night when he felt the first icy fear of living without the woman he loved since their first days of college. While Aaron sat looking at the pictures of Krista he always carried with him, I placed the flowers where he thought she died. It was a gesture that felt completely unsatisfying in expressing the terrible loss of her life. Jim and I sat side by side on the mountain. Holding each other, we tried to comprehend this truth that our beloved daughter breathed her last breath in this ravine so far from home. I saw Aaron's bewildering pain, thought of the unborn children we would never know, grieved for Jefferson and Susan, a brother and sister who will lose a lifetime of familial friendship, and her soul-friends, whose dreams of the future entwined with hers in wanting to create a more compassionate world.

Then Jim got up and found a tree trunk to carve. With a Swiss Army knife, he etched "Krista—May 20, 1998." Her biology-loving heart might question this tree scarring, but we assumed she would understand her historian-father's need for tangible remembrance. I was unable to speak, except to say to the wind, "I cannot believe that one careless bus driver could kill so much love."

When other parents tell of their wrestling with returning to the places of significance in their child's life, their responses vary immensely. For some, visiting the site of death proves essential, much as we see families in the news needing to visit the ocean or land where a plane crashed. For Patti McClary, whose daughter Katie died in Durham, North Carolina, when a city bus struck her, it was not only essential to visit the site; she also planned a return trip on the year anniversary. "I just had a compelling need to stand on the street in remembrance of her last moments," she said.

"It's the last place I wanted to be," said another mother as she told me about the remote country road in Nebraska where her seventeen-year-old son died in a car accident. "I've *never* gone near it."

The same diverse response can happen between husbands and wives as they contemplate revisiting places where shared family memories have been positive or important to their child. What may comfort one creates distress for the other.

I was unable to speak, except to say to the wind, "I cannot believe that one careless bus driver could kill so much love."

George Girvin, a retired surgeon, lost his thirty-four-year-old son Matthew in a helicopter crash while serving with the United Nations in Mongolia. George found solace as he worked on eighty acres of land and two small homesteads that he developed with his son. One little cabin sat on the upper site where this busy surgeon found time to relax with summer picnics or winter toboggan runs when his four boys were growing up. When Matthew, a graduate from Emory University in International Public Health, completed a health project in China at thirty-three, he came home. He thought it was just for a few months before taking a UNICEF position in Mongolia. This time extended to over a year, so he worked with his dad on remodeling the cabin of his childhood. Side by side they began dry walling, painting, taping, rewiring, and plumbing, all new skills he learned. "He really took ownership and saw this as his home when he'd return to America. It was really fun to work as partners alongside an adult son," remembers George. "He was the teacher, and I knew even then that this was a rare opportunity to know my son in a new way." Matthew also had a strong interest in forest management, so they planted new seedlings of ponderosa pine and fir, plus thinned tamarack and larch, and transplanted hemlock from native forests.

After Matthew's death, his father began going to their Tower Mountain farm several times a week. "I felt I was going to his place and continuing to care for something he loved." Earlier Matthew had brought home a tree sapling from Mongolia and transplanted it on the property. He then covered it with pine boughs for protection. "We were looking for a place to put a memorial marker, and two months later we found the little seedling had survived." So they built a cairn of rocks in the Mongolian tradition that overlooks their cabin and a large vegetable garden. "These ancient cairns are on the trails up the mountainside passes. Hikers add another rock and give a prayer of thanks when they arrive . . . called OVOO. We had a pyramid rock from Mongolia and had his name etched on it," said his father. "I can go there, see his tree, and remember him. And give thanks for his being in our lives. It's so quiet, with red tail hawks, raven, the creatures that Matt would talk to and I envision they are his messengers. I just like to go up and look around because the land is so alive."

Not so for his wife, Lila. "I find it almost impossible to go there for long. These wonderful family memories still create too much pain." They understand this difference in one another and respect it.

Sometimes returning to a painful place simply isn't a choice. Doug and Sharon Clegg, whose son jumped from his third-floor apartment window, had to go to the death site to clean out his apartment. "Our pastor warned us that this would be a brutal day," recalls Sharon, so they brought seven family members. Stephen had struggled for years with bipolar disorder with psychotic episodes and alcohol abuse. His behavior during these episodes led to a prison term and the loss of his marriage. Most painful for Stephen was an order restraining him from seeing his two daughters since they were one and three years old. "He was working hard to get his life back together to be able to see his girls," remembers Sharon. "He was attending the community college with a goal to be a social worker helping people with mental challenges like he had. He was even getting straight A's."

They had never seen his new apartment, but heard it was in a good neighborhood east of Seattle. The detective said his apartment was "neat as a pin" and that he had left no suicide note. A friend told them Steve admitted he had recently gone off his medicines because he didn't want any more chemicals in his body.

"When we walked into his apartment, everything spoke of his desire to get healthy," said Sharon. "His desktop had his workout schedule and weight training plan, the books on his shelves were on physical and spiritual health, and there were bananas and fresh meat in the refrigerator . . . making us feel that he hadn't contemplated suicide for a long time." On his bedside was a handwritten statement of faith with his signature. They weren't sure if he had copied this or written it himself. They also discovered a box of letters he'd written to each of his daughters on their birthday for the past four years, letters he hoped to give them someday. He wanted them to know of his constant love when they reunited.

As the family began to sort through his clothing and place them in boxes, they would ask Sharon, "Mom, should we save this?" She found herself unable to make decisions. "Right now I want Steve so bad, I can't give away anything or make discerning choices." She stopped helping and went into his bedroom to lie down on his bed. "His scent was so real, when I put the comforter that I had made for him around me, I just sobbed and sobbed until I fell asleep exhausted. When I awoke two and a half hours later, I was in much better shape."

To this day, she is grateful she went. "You need to feel the pain. But there was also a sweetness to it, to see how beautifully neat he kept it, to see the family pictures around the rooms, to see the hope his choice of books represented. I wouldn't have missed this for anything."

A year later, they traveled back to Seattle for a family event and inadvertently found themselves staying at a motel that was very close to his old apartment. "This was the last place I ever wanted to be again, but it turned out to be a good thing. Doug and I grieved again, but the area had lost its power," recalls Sharon. "I found I was no longer afraid of the neighborhood. It was one more step in healing. There is not a finish line on healing and I can accept this fact. I love life, but there will always be this deep sadness."

A year later, the Clegg's actually returned to this motel and neighborhood by choice. "We could be there with ease, which was a significant sign to us in the healing that is happening."

"It was one more step in healing.
There is not a finish line on healing and
I can accept this fact. I love life, but there
will always be this deep sadness."
—*Sharon Clegg*

Parents who lose young children find themselves faced with different challenges and decisions.

"When our seven-year-old was alive, I use to volunteer in his classroom," said Cheryl Hillis, whose healthy, sports-loving little boy Joshua Dean (JD) died suddenly one afternoon after a game of pick-up basketball. After a while, she tried volunteering in his classroom again because the children showed such friendship for her son. "It was far too painful to be with children his age . . . even to see his desk," she recalls. Instead, she volunteered in the main office, now seeing children from kindergarten to sixth grade. "Somehow this worked. It felt good to be back in the school he loved so much and that loved him."

When a child dies who still lived at home, parents face a myriad of emotions surrounding the intimate places in their child's life. "To this day, I have kept my son's room intact," said one mother I met at a cemetery a few years after the death of her child. "The best guidance I ever received was that there is no one way, or right way to grieve. To others, not utilizing my son's room for another purpose seems strange, but I will know when it is time," she remarked confidently. She still finds comfort sitting or reading in the place he loved and tending to his country grave site.

For other parents, the site of an empty crib or a child's favorite toys proves too visual a reminder of their terrible loss. Anne Morrow Lindbergh, wife of America's famous aviator, writes the following in her journal four months after their eighteen-month-old son was kidnapped. Shortly after they paid a ransom, he was found murdered.

> Sunday, July 17, 1932 . . . I am in a kind of stupor now about the baby. I do not go up to his room or look at his things or write in his record or go over the pictures. I feel in a kind of hopeless numbness. He is gone. I can't get him back that way or any other way. He is just gone. There is nothing to do. How futile to try to hang on to him by these scraps. How futile to hope that a miniature would have some of him—and even so, what comfort would it be in the face of that complete loss. The picture gets dimmer and I, hopeless, do not fight the inevitable.[1]

What I heard most from parents was their strong need to trust their instincts and sense of timing; no one else can fully understand. "One of the great enemies of grief is giving oneself a timetable," says Jerry Sittser who has counseled with many people in the years since his catastrophic loss. "This means you are letting someone else determine your story. It's the same problem with assuming there are 'stages' in grief because when something comes back, like overpowering waves of anger or despair or loss, it's easy to think something is wrong. But in fact, major loss often triggers earlier periods of loss that finally need to be attended to." Nineteen years after the death of his four-year-old daughter, Diana Jane, Jerry's fiancée casually mentioned, "I didn't know Jamie was Diane Jane's Sunday School teacher." To his surprise, he broke down and sobbed, grieving for his four-year-old again. "It triggered something . . . grief will surface and recede all of our lives."

Sometimes what is easier, some parents tell me, is to visit the *kind* of places their child liked, such as a trip to the ocean, a baseball park, a stage play, a hike in a national forest, or a visit to the zoo. It's not as painful as remembering your child in a specific place, but there is pleasure in knowing this place would be loved by your child. Barbara Grigsby lost her son Larry after years of debilitating treatments for cancer before his death at twenty-two. Barbara and her husband knew that one of Larry's favorite pleasures was eating a good hamburger. "In the first couple of years after his death, whenever my husband and I traveled, it became a ritual to find the best hamburger in a town," recalls Barbara. "It gave us a way to sit and savor memories together of Larry."

Visiting Krista's accident site gave me no such sense of peace. As we scrambled up the hillside, our hearts felt unimaginably heavier. I began to wonder if our friends might be right. Was coming to her world really a wise choice after all? Yet, however difficult, touching the land and adding our tears to the exact mountain crevasse that claimed our daughter's life seemed essential.

Chapter 5

ALLOWING TIME FOR THE LONG
SEASON OF SORROW

*You're not doing nothing. Being fully open to your grief is
probably the hardest work you'll do in your whole life.*

—A wise man's counsel to a woman who lamented that sitting and
staring out the window was all she wanted to do after a profound loss

∽∾

QUESTION: CAN WE RESIST AMERICA'S "MOURNING-AVOIDANT"
CULTURE AND FIND HEALING BY TRUSTING THE TIME AND
WORK GRIEF TAKES?

In the maelstrom of sorrow there is an inevitable temptation to want to rush through these painful days. Or others want you to "move on" as if one gets over a death easily. The Oregon poet William Stafford captures this reality in his poem "Consolations." One section includes:

"The broken part heals even stronger than the rest,"
they say. But that takes awhile.
And, "Hurry up," the whole world says.
They tap their feet. And it still hurts on rainy
afternoons when the same absent sun
gives no sign it will ever come back.[1]

If giving ourselves a timetable is one of the great enemies of grief, the other enemy is distraction observe many grief counselors. There are lots of varieties, whether television, hobbies, alcohol, business . . . anything, because we don't want to face such overwhelming pain. In Stephen Levine's book *Unattended Sorrow: Recovering from Loss and Reviving the Heart,* he draws from his experiences as a counselor with Vietnam veterans, Holocaust survivors, and others coping with death. He finds that feelings of loss don't go away. They just go deeper. Even more, the American approach to burying our feelings or trying to protect ourselves from pain has significant consequences, often leading to other problems and a "narrowing of life."[2]

Our confidence that we could make life happen as we wish, or our belief in unquestioned expectations lies wounded. Unattended, Levine finds grief will manifest in many unexpected ways. It disturbs sleep, infects dreams, and saps energy. This may lead to emotional distancing, a closing off of part of ourselves, or clinical depression. For others, it can lead to addictions of all sorts, whether overeating, excessive drinking, drugs, anything to mask the pain. It's like a low-grade fever with a long fading trust in life itself, a kind of general malaise or hopelessness that causes us to lose heart. He also observed that sometimes an immediate loss triggers earlier ungrieved losses, such as childhood traumas, family divorces, feelings of failure or rejection, the bruises of life. To find peace in our sorrow, Levine counsels that one needs the courage to face the pain.

When families stay silent after the death of a child, it also has inevitable implications for siblings. "My parents never talked about my little sister that died in childbirth," recalls Mark Terrell, a man nearing his forties who founded an inner-city ministry for homeless youth. "But last year, after the death of a young man in our program, the way Erica had been obliterated from our family really troubled me. I did some research and found her gravesite. I was the first in our family to ever visit it," he told me with tears. He recalled one summer when he worked with his dad at a paper mill. "We drove by the cemetery every day, but she was never talked about and I didn't feel free to ask. I learned early to stuff a lot of my emotions. Her unspoken death profoundly affected my life growing up as an only child." With guidance from a counselor, he's now written her a letter to express his loss as a big brother.

. . . sometimes an immediate loss triggers earlier ungrieved losses, such as childhood traumas, family divorces, feelings of failure or rejection, the bruises of life.
—*Stephen Levine*

Levine sees great hope for persons willing, like Mark, to face and attend pain, even if years have passed. He observes that trying to protect ourselves from pain limits us—pushes away all that we love. This leaves us feeling isolated, unable to express the depth of those feelings. But if we stay open to mercy and tap the resources of the heart, we can regain the strength to love, the power to forgive, and discover a path toward peace after loss. We can trust the heart has room for it all . . . the suffering as well as the joys.

> But if we stay open to mercy and tap the resources of the heart, we can regain the strength to love, the power to forgive, and discover a path toward peace after loss.

It takes courage to go near where we don't want to be. But as Nicholas Wolterstorff insisted in his book *Lament for a Son*, "I will not look away from Eric's death. . . . I owe that to him and to God, to look death and pain in the face."[3] An honest account of his questions and pain, Wolterstorff describes his searing desolation after the mountain climbing death of his twenty-five-year-old son. Twelve years afterward, when people asked him if the grief was as intense, he said, "No, the wound is no longer raw. But it has not disappeared. That is as it should be. If he was worth loving, he is worth grieving over. Grief is existential testimony to the worth of the one loved. That worth abides. So I own my grief. I do not try to put it behind me, to get over it, to forget it. I do not try to dis-own it."[4] I read his book years before Krista died, and it was one of the early books I turned to after her death.

Being open to facing our grief shaped our decision to go to Bolivia and to meet the people Krista knew and was growing to love. Prior to our leaving, many friends and family had given us presents to offer solace for our loss. This natural outpouring of kindness is often experienced by parents and siblings during the harsh early months. These gifts of poetry, Krista's e-mails, old photographs, "Young Love" lilies, and a St. Francis statue for the garden all nurtured our spirits.

Because of such kindnesses, we decided to carry small

books to the three Bolivian families who also lost someone in this bus accident. The inside pages included spaces for photographs, drawings, and writing. We imagined that their friends and families could write about their loved one while these memories remained fresh. This could then be passed down through the family over the generations, keeping memories alive.

We arrived in Comarapa late in the afternoon. "It's the armpit of Bolivia," said Chris, referring to the constant swirl of dust. But with over three thousand people here, we knew Aaron and Krista had enjoyed this nearest "big city" as they settled into their remote community. At the diner where they shared their last meal together, Aaron talked to the owner about the other surviving families. The restaurant owner shared his sorrow and shock and then commented sadly, "I even remember you ordered an egg sandwich that evening before Krista and you boarded the bus."

During the night of the accident, Aaron met a little toddler with a stick protruding from his bleeding forehead. "His mother also died in the accident, but I know he lived," explained Aaron. The restaurant owner knew the families and called a young boy to lead us down the labyrinth of dusty alleyways to their homes.

The toddler's father, Senor de Velarde, answered the first door while holding the child in his arms. Startled to see three North Americans, he invited us in. A tall muscular man, he was dressed in black, the tradition for a year of mourning in Bolivia. We learned he was an educated agronomist working for the government. Tears welled in his eyes as he told us of his wife, also a teacher, and the three children, now motherless. We heard other children crying from a back room. "We had just celebrated her thirtieth birthday and our son's second birthday," he explained. "My mother is now helping with the kids." He and Aaron talked for a while in

Spanish as these two widowers worked hard to understand each other. Aaron turned to share the conversation with us in English. "He helped bring Krista up from the accident site on a mat."

An MCC staff member told us earlier how carefully and tenderly her body had been brought up on the steep mountain slope. I felt grateful to this grieving husband, who in the shock of losing his wife, still took time to help our unknown daughter. He thanked us for the book as he and Aaron said good-bye. These two men from different lands clearly felt united in their sorrow of losing a loved wife. We returned to the hotel acutely aware that our loss was linked forever with other Bolivians.

We woke on Sunday morning to belching trucks and crowing roosters as farmers arrived to set up for their lively market day. Each week, families joined together in transport trucks from the surrounding countryside to buy and sell goods, produce, and animals. Aaron and Krista usually joined their neighbors in this rural rhythm, often riding along with the live chickens, pigs, or goats beside them. We strolled along the dirt streets now transformed by a feast of farm-fresh fruits, vegetables, and grains. The vendors' artistic display of gigantic green peppers and lettuces, varieties of yuccas and purple potatoes, quinoa, vine-ripe tomatoes, and spices reminded me of Seattle's Pike Place market, another favorite place for Krista and Aaron and our family.

"You've got to try Api," insisted Aaron as we found the corner stall. "It was Krista's favorite drink. It's made of purple corn, cinnamon, and sugar . . . she loved it." I take a sip and the aroma brings memories of the hot spiced wine and apple cider brewed for guests in our home each winter as she grew up.

On the street we met two American men from a nearby town, an unusual sight in this non-tourist region. They worked in an American school for children of missionaries and knew of Krista's death. In conversation, we learned that years ago the older man lost a sixteen-year-old son in an accident while on furlough in America. He kindly sought to console us. He meant well, but when he proudly said, "My wife was a realist and started getting rid of his clothing the day after he died," I recoiled. I resisted this tone of "get on with it" as life's tidy way of dealing with death. Was this another kind of America's one-minute manager lifestyle, only now its one-minute grief?

What's real about that? I wondered silently as I thought about Krista redesigning my long-stored wedding dress for her own marriage. I found myself saddened by his understanding of his wife's response, a decision most likely made in the midst of profound shock. When his voice escalated into preaching, we signaled one another it was time to split.

I resisted this tone of "get on with it" as life's tidy way of dealing with death. Was this another kind of America's one-minute manager lifestyle, only now its one-minute grief?

Unbeknownst to him, it was this question—how do I prepare for an absence the size of Krista—that lies at the heart of my own search. How can we sustain the memory of her rare spirit in a healthy and non-obsessive way that nourishes her family and friends? How do we fill the broken crack where such raw hurt lives now? I only knew it couldn't be instant.

I thought about one of Krista's last e-mails about the importance Bolivian culture places on relationships, both with the living and the dead.

> I'm learning a lot about our task-driven culture versus a relationship based culture. Family is definitely the priority here (while often expressed sexist), but definitely a priority.

Why don't we live in a culture where you take two weeks to honor the dead and console the living? Why don't we leave work to be with a friend in the hospital, instead of making our dutiful visitation for 15 minutes? From the development standpoint, when we come into a community and focus on the work, the task, the achievements and not invest into the relationships, our being there is almost worthless in their eyes.

And I thought about the scrapbooks made by MCC volunteers and friends, and the vibrant poems and letters of memories sent to us. These gifts were all efforts to keep Krista's memory alive and strong in the absence of her presence. I know how much we have needed these tangible expressions of her life, a bounty of grace given to ease this grief.

Other parents told me similar stories of this oppressive burden of rushed grief. "I ran into an acquaintance in the grocery store a few months after our twenty-five-year-old daughter Katie died," recalls Patti McClary. "In an accusatory tone, she said to me, 'We invite you to things and you don't show up. You never want to come. Get over it! It's time.'" Comments like this can almost freeze parents into further retrenchment.

Knowing one never "gets over" the death of a child does not mean one can't eventually live again with an expanded heart and vibrant hope that life can still resound with meaning.

To attempt this is an illusionary exercise in positive thinking. Nor do parents long to "get over" the love they carry for their child. Rev. John Perkins, a national leader on racial reconciliation and development, recalled how pivotal it was that he had heard another father's story shortly before his forty-year-old son Spencer died of a heart attack. "I was so glad to have heard Rev. John Huffman, a pastor friend, insist that he never wanted "to get over" his daughter, a beautiful woman who died of cancer shortly after graduating from Princeton University. Perkins believes this prepared him to live with sorrow. "I've learned to release what I can, and embrace the pain that stays."

Knowing one never "gets over" the death of a child does not mean one can't eventually live again with an expanded heart and vibrant hope that life can still resound with meaning. Dr. Alan Wolfelt, as director of The Center for Loss and Life Transition has companioned thousands of persons facing the wilderness of grief. He believes that hope emerges when people make a commitment and intention to heal. He encourages people to be open and attentive to their pain, but he also recommends "dosing" your pain. "You must allow yourself to 'dose' the pain—feel it in small waves then allow it to retreat until you are ready for the next wave."[5] Even years later, he finds people experience unexpected "grief bursts"—like a rogue ocean wave that pulls your feet right out from under you.

Not desiring "to get over" Krista brought us far from home into the Bolivian river valley that enchanted her heart, a land abundant with giant cactus so different from our Northwest Ponderosa Pines. Over dinner, after visiting the families in Comarapa, Aaron began reminiscing over his final hours with Krista. "The irony is that morning we rode our motorcycles into a distant town to bring condolences and a hand-made card to a man who had lost his son in an accident," recalled Aaron. "Krista carried Choclo in an aguayo, the traditional all-purpose weavings used to carry babies, vegetables, or bundles on women's backs. It fascinated our friends since dogs tend to be treated like scum here, certainly never carried. She loved this puppy so much; we brought him with us whenever we could. He snuggled on our laps before the bus flew over the cliff." Pausing, Aaron looked away into the distant mountains. Lost in thought, he prepared to face a cascade of memories when we returned to their cherished adobe home in Bañado the next day. I couldn't imagine what tomorrow would bring.

Chapter 6

RECEIVING GRACE
ALONG THE JOURNEY

*Don't get me wrong. Grief sucks; it really does. Unfortunately,
though, avoiding it robs us of Life, of the now, of the sense
of living spirit. . . . The bad news is that whatever you use to
keep the pain at bay robs you of the flecks and nuggets
of gold that feeling grief will give you.*

—Anne LaMott, *Traveling Mercies: Some Thoughts on Faith*

❧

QUESTION: CAN WE RECOGNIZE THE SMALL TREASURES THAT
WILL HELP US HEAL?

When Anne LaMott speaks of "the flecks and nuggets of gold" that feeling grief will give you, this seems almost unfathomable in the earliest acute days of shattering loss. But some say the Latin symbol Au for the chemical element of gold means the "glow of sunrise" or "rising dawn," alluding to a shimmer of hope. Over and over, parents spoke of such moments of hope and grace that gave them strength and courage to rise and face another day.

Because of Krista's death, we have become friends with several other parents who have lost teenagers or young adult children, some during international experiences. Most hunger to know more of their maturing child's world.

Over and over, parents spoke of such moments
of hope and grace that gave them strength and
courage to rise and face another day.

Not too long after Krista's death, Etta, a sixteen-year-old Rotary International Exchange student from Port Orchard, Washington, also died in a bus accident in Bolivia. A dynamic, exuberant free spirit, she always made deep friendships because of her natural love for others and zany love of life. The Bolivians in Montero also loved her spirit and grieved for her family. After beginning a project in Etta's honor, the Montero Rotary Club and the Salesian priests invited the family to visit.

"After her death, at first I just wanted to crawl in a hole and die. But when this opportunity came to visit, we're so thankful we went," said her mother, Pennye Nixon. The project was a dining hall, a "commedor" that would feed one hundred impoverished children. They wanted permission to name it after Etta.

Profoundly moved after encountering the poverty that Etta saw daily, in 2003 they began a partnership with Bolivians called Etta Projects. "It also provided a unity in our blended family, as her father, her stepfather, and I worked together to develop support for this." The project expanded in Montero to provide a daycare and preschool, plus job training and household management for mothers, and evolved to include rural communities.

Pennye noticed that both Etta's stepfather and dad grieved differently from her. "They were much more ready to deal with the outside world in a proactive way, while I needed almost two to three years. Her father speaks Spanish and could organize events and that proved healing for him. I needed more space," recalls Pennye.

"But death can bring fear," admits Pennye. "Eventually, I had to decide to either wilt or die or to be open to the opportunities that evolved from Etta's death, including the willingness to grow. There needed to be some meaning emerge instead of the constant confusion." Pennye, a family therapist, now works full time on Etta Projects in partnership with Bolivians to assist impoverished women and families in several villages. "When I've struggled with meaning, I've come to an ultimate sense in the importance of kindness in life. There's a poem by Naomi Shihab Nye, a poet with a Palestinian father and American mother, who has a lifelong interest in the similarities and differences between cultures. It has been pivotal for me."

Kindness

Before you know what kindness really is
you must lose things,
feel the future dissolve in a moment
like salt in a weakened broth.
What you held in your hand,
what you counted and carefully saved,
all this must go so you know how desolate the landscape can be
between the regions of kindness.

How you ride and ride
thinking the bus will never stop,
the passengers eating maize and chicken
will stare out the window forever.

Before you learn the tender gravity of kindness,
you must travel where the Indian in a white poncho
lies dead by the side of the road.
You must see how this could be you,
how he too was someone
who journeyed through the night with plans
and the simple breath that kept him alive.

Before you know kindness as the deepest thing inside,
you must know sorrow as the other deepest thing.
You must wake with sorrow.
You must speak to it till your voice
catches the thread of all sorrows
and you see the size of the cloth.

Then it is only kindness that makes sense anymore,
only kindness that ties your shoes
and sends you out into the day to mail letters and purchase
     bread,
only kindness that raises its head from the crowd of the world
     to say
it is I you have been looking for,
and then goes with you everywhere
like a shadow or a friend.[1]

Grieving parents describe other nuggets of gold they discover about their child after death. Sometimes reading books their children loved or the journals in which they wrote offer insights. "Our son, Stephen, had an amazing capacity for friendship," recalled Dick Baker. "We found a book on friendship in his bookcase titled *Friendship as Sacrament* and I felt I understood his priorities even more as I read this." After a doctor lost his son, an English major, he spent a year reading his son's college textbooks. As a father fascinated by science, he wanted to understand his son's joy and passion for Elizabethan literature.

Our visit to Krista and Aaron's Bolivian home also gave flecks of gold that surprised us. After our night in Comarapa, the next morning we began the fifteen-kilometer ascent up a twisting primitive mountain road that then dips down to a delightful river valley. Now the dry season, the verdant green hillsides Aaron and Krista knew in the rainy season had turned a drab brown. Swirling dust replaced their earlier battles with mud and an impassable flooding river. Forty-foot spiny cactus and prolific scrub cacti testify to the desert-like terrain. Yet, as we descended toward the Rio Comarapa, an elaborate mosaic of irrigated fields created a fertile oasis of bountiful crops.

We saw a farmer plowing with two oxen, tilling fields much like his ancestors. The community of Bañado de la Cruz has no village but includes around fifty families who live in subsistence farms spread along the river, often at great distances from one another. These were the families who Aaron and Krista worked with through an agricultural cooperative and women's community groups. Krista also helped start libraries in two nearby towns. "She was here such a short three months. Will they even miss her?" I wondered aloud.

Grieving parents describe other nuggets of gold they discover about their child after death.

"Let me tell you a story," answered Chris, our translator who was the first MCC volunteer to live in the area before Aaron and Krista arrived. "Shortly after her death, I met the husband of one of the women in the community. He'd found out about Krista's death first and just dreaded telling his wife. He told me she cried for three days . . . she said she felt abandoned." We also learned that when the women in the community group heard of her death, they rented a truck to go into Comarapa where they thought her body would be returned. "This was clearly an extravagant gesture," said Chris. "Knowing Aaron had no family nearby; they probably planned to prepare her body for burial. When they discovered she had been brought to Santa Cruz, none could afford the eight-hour trip."

How much I will miss our rich conversations around the dinner table or over coffee as she tried to merge her absorbing interests in women's literature, politics, and biology.

More than any part of this odyssey, it was their valley home and community of Bolivian friends I most longed to see. I recalled her disappointment when she first saw the one-room adobe home connected to the community center. *We romanticize adobe in America,* she wrote, admitting to her "borderline depression" at the sight. *In fact, I live in a mud and straw house with a little cement which has been baked in the sun and looks like it's going to disintegrate in the first rain. It looks like crap."* Without electricity or plumbing, they needed to use a dry latrine and outdoor bucket for showers. They gathered water from a distant spring and the river.

However, within days Krista began to love their new home as Aaron and she gave it their own touches. She especially liked looking out the spacious windows overlooking the bucolic view of farmlands and mountains, and listening to the sounds of the river from the porch hammock. To us she wrote, *I love it here and am increasingly content and happy with my new home. I love that there are more donkeys, pigs, and goats roaming the road than cars. I love taking hikes. I love getting strong carrying water. And I love what being here does for our marriage.*

"I need to go in alone at first," said Aaron. In a little while, he invited us into their home now ablaze with candlelight.

Rather than the cold chill I feared, stepping into their one-room home filled me with a warm sense of Krista's presence everywhere. Exquisite Andean tapestries hung on the white plastered walls near their "bedroom" section. A vibrant hand-woven bedspread and pillows created an artful space. A red enamel tea kettle, bought at the local market, sat on the gas stove. A blue-patterned tablecloth brightened up the corner.

I browsed at the books on their over-stacked bookshelves. Fedor Dostoevsky, Toni Morrison, Carlos Fuentes, Barbara Kingsolver, Carl Gustav Jung, John Grisham, Michael Creighton, J. R. R. Tolkien, Brother Lawrence, Thomas Merton, Gabriel Garcia Marquez, and Eugene Peterson, among others. What a feast of friends for the long nights of quiet so rare in American society. Other books spoke of their practical work, such as *The Complete Bee Manual, Building Dry Latrines, Where There Are No Doctors.* I picked up Toni Morrison's *Tar Baby,* one of the last books she read, and remember Krista's lively, thoughtful mind. How much I will miss our rich conversations around the dinner table or over coffee as she tried to merge her absorbing interests in women's literature, politics, and biology. Aaron showed me a birthday note she wrote him. At the end, she signed it, "'For a man who loves a good book, will love a good woman.' Krista to Aaron."

He also showed me one of his last love letters written to Krista when they needed to spend a few days apart.

> I was reviewing our photos when I came across these two that caused me to pause. In both I was struck by just how incredibly beautiful you are. . . . You're so close to me, but when we are apart, you become like a dream or something I only longed to have and now can only experience in memories. . . . I think your beauty must spring from your loveliness, everything else that makes me love and desire you.

Then a few paragraphs later, he closes with the words, "I am so lucky to have you as my life friend, partner, and lover—my wife."

About then Chris told us we needed to move all the furniture. "Stay outside while I spray the baseboard for scorpions, tarantulas, and vinchucas. We need to do this before we can sleep safely. A bite from the vinchuca, a common beetle, can cause the dreaded Chagas disease that afflicts over 25 percent of Bolivia's population and leads to a slow death." Then Aaron mentioned, "We found fifteen dead scorpions after the last spray," and I'm reminded that what looks romantic harbors dangers to unwary residents. "Look at Krista's tarantulas," said Aaron. He showed me two jars with giant spiders that she had preserved. Even dead, their black furry bodies and legs caused me to wince. Yet I relished her sense of curiosity, alive since childhood, to all living creatures.

Aaron concocted a fresh spaghetti sauce on their gas stove. Soon an aroma of basil, garlic, and tomatoes filled their one-room home. A small pantry shelf held the few ingredients that can survive without refrigeration: plastic containers of flour, sugar, cocoa, olive oil, powdered milk, tea, and spices. "We learned to cook with just about twenty ingredients in the house," explained Aaron. "In America, it used to be that if I was missing something, like mushrooms, I wanted to rush to the store to create the perfect dish. Here I was learning how to be content with what we had. I was learning to live without."

My heart almost stopped as I heard our passionate, handsome son-in-law chatting about living without mushrooms. I've seen his pain as he learned to live without his mom, Linda, who died four years earlier of breast cancer. Now he has lost his wife, who infused his days with such radiance, and he's only twenty-five. How will he choose to live without Krista?

Later in the evening, Aaron found her journal and began reading aloud to us. Listening, we gained a sense of how Bañado nourished her spirit of adventure. A long, early entry told of their move from Santa Cruz to Bañado on a transport truck:

February 22, 1998

We piled in with Chris, Philip, 2 cats, a puppy, all our stuff and about 20 people and their belongings. While fun at first, it quickly became cold and then ultimately freezing. . . . The bumps would slam my body into the 18 cement squatters as our thin blanket slowly worked its ways from our toes and fingers. I doubt I have ever been that uncomfortable in my life for that many hours. What should have taken 7 hours took 11, and I'm sure the driver was drinking at each stop, in addition to paying off the officials for not having a license.

MCC gave Aaron and Krista two Honda motorbikes for transportation, and Chris had coached her on how to ride the treacherous terrain, avoiding spiny cactus, eroded sections, jolting rocks, loose pigs, and cow dung. In a culture where domestic abuse prevails, her first week meeting families in Bañado posed problems. She writes:

As I learn the art of motorcycle driving, I manage to crash twice. The first time in a hole over an irrigation canal and the second time in a mud hole. I am left with a bump/bruise on my chin and two enormous bruises on my thighs. It kills to ride again, but I have to learn. My knee is all scraped up and I seriously look like some abused wife or rape victim—it's awful and because they don't ask, I feel like I have to explain my clumsiness as we meet each new family so they don't think Aaron beats me.

As I listened, I remembered her funny letter saying riding motorcycles was like being in control of some sick carnival ride, but how she couldn't wait to show her gutsy brother Jefferson her new Evel Knievel talents.

Krista was the first female volunteer in Bañado, and the women welcomed her with generous hearts. Distant neighbors often brought them gifts of eggs, mangoes, tomatoes, potatoes, mandarins, and even valued cherimoya fruit. Aaron read an entry from the end of the first week where she summed up life in this new land.

> So within a week, I've visited all the families that are in the project, fell in the river, crashed motorcycles twice, washed clothes in the river, played soccer, attended a meeting of the community and government, and figured out if there is bread for sale or not, baked green peppers with the women's group, received corn, potatoes, onions, corn flour; filled the pee container twice, swept and swept again, baked cookies twice, lentils twice, carried water past a "bad" bull, and got diarrhea. I thank God for . . . the women who get along, the stars, fear, answered prayer and the peacefulness of space.

She ended with a notation on Psalm 84:5 where she transposed the reference to man to include women. *How blessed is the woman whose strength is in Thee.*

Then Aaron discovered a tape that Krista made for our 30th wedding anniversary, but hadn't yet mailed. "A creation from your creation," she wrote in a note. Her buoyant voice permeated the room as we listened closely to her tales of their first few weeks. It included stories of hosting high school students who visited from a Saskatchewan church. This first work project helped villagers build eleven dry latrines, a low-tech-high-sanitation toilet.

"The families fed them and were incredibly generous. To see twenty North Americans working on latrines with the Bolivian families, building relationships and learning about another culture, was wonderful," she remarked with obvious pleasure in her voice. "For a fifteen-year-old to realize not everyone has MTV can be life shaping."

She ended the hour-long tape saying, "I'm in awe of the beauty here. I love life and am thankful you gave it to me."

Hearing the joie de vivre in her voice seemed so natural, especially in the way we talked about anything and everything.

I felt that if I turned my head I might see her walk through the front door.

The next day we walked down the lane to the nearby school house, the only other community building. The women worked all morning fixing a lunch to welcome us, a generous feast of chicken, rice, lettuce, and tomato salad. Their quiet love and sadness for Aaron was immediately evident, each offering him condolences. Several of the young mothers, with babies slung on their backs, looked far younger than Krista. These were the women who initiated the dry latrine project and welcomed and fed Canadian high school volunteers in their homes. "We will never forget her," many said to us, as their tears flowed freely.

We gave them a framed picture of Krista and her beloved dog, Choclo, taken in one of the women's corn fields, and thanked them for their many kindnesses to Aaron and Krista. Through Lorie, our interpreter, we told them of the small waterfall and pond built in the backyard and our desire to have words engraved on rocks that friends felt described her. "Did they have any they want us to add?" we asked.

"Alegria!" responded her neighbor Dionisea immediately. Women murmured their assent to this Spanish word for joyful. Each woman eagerly joined in words of remembrance. *A good friend, helpful, funny, beautiful, smiling, a queen, a hard worker, a lover of children and animals, so kind, so encouraging.* The genuine affection these twelve women held for an American woman demonstrated the power of mutual openness and respect, a power that allowed women to bridge the boundaries of culture. They sensed this blossoming friendship and clearly grieved for their loss.

Then, two of the women told of dreams they had of Krista, a very personal gift to us.

"In my dream, I met Krista one day at the river," said Nikolasia, a young mother nursing a baby. "Krista, I thought you were dead," she remembered saying.

"No, I'm fine."

"But how can you be fine if you're dead?"

"They took my heart in a box to the north and fixed it," explained Krista. "I'm fine. But Aaron's not doing well."

How true, I thought, knowing Aaron's searing loneliness.

Then another woman told of a similar dream where Krista came to visit her at her home.

"I thought you plunged over the cliff in the micro-bus," she said when startled by Krista's presence.

"No, I'm fine."

"But you are supposed to be dead."

"No, I'm just fine. Look at me!" More tears came to the women as their friend told her story.

Afterward, Lorie and Chris expressed surprise at their openness. "These are very private women. They usually don't talk this openly even among themselves."

I wondered if the heart of Krista's work was giving isolated women a sense of value. They could dream together to make changes in their world. With no libraries, no health care, no fresh water, no refrigeration, no electricity, no local schooling after sixth grade, they were starting to dream of possibilities. Their next project was building a separate meeting place for women, a room of their own. "She was dynamite," insisted one teacher in Chilon, the small town where she rode her motorcycle to help launch a local library. "Her dynamic presence will be so missed."

I wondered if the heart of Krista's work was giving isolated women a sense of value. They could dream together to make changes in their world.

On our way to the airport at the end of this trip, a large piece of old cardboard flew onto the grill of the taxi. Flapping wildly in the wind, it forced our driver to pull off the freeway.

We assumed he would just throw it on the ground. Instead, he carefully placed it in the trunk. "It's a gift from the road," I said to Jim, intrigued by how the driver saw treasure in what another would call trash. He climbed back into the front seat beaming and announced, "*Un regallo de la calle.*" Lining the trunk, he used this "gift from the road" to protect his taxi from luggage damage.

How many small treasures we have been given in this painful pilgrimage, a trip we once considered not taking. For the past two weeks we have been seeing the final months in the beautifully textured life of our daughter. Her actions lived out her expressed desire for a holistic faith, sharing in God's love to all creation. And as she showed this love of all God's land and peoples, her spirit touched Bolivians from many walks of life. Bañado peasant women, educated Andean Network activists, MCC community volunteers, teachers, farmers, children, even the neighborhood dogs that claimed her porch as home.

With the wind in her hair and a beloved husband at her side, she flew with zest on a motorbike across high mountain terrain to serve three communities. She worked alongside others for basic things: a decent latrine, libraries and literacy for children, a sense of worth and community for women, a home where love dwelled. These were simple acts, done with great devotion, in an unknown river valley. Yet because she was never burdened by a false sense of her own importance, she kept the joy. Seeing how her joy touched others in such a brief time gave us a reservoir of joy in the cup of sorrow, a gift that has endured.

As Jim and I flew back to the States the next day, I knew we had been blessed by this trip into terrible beauty. I sensed the gifts offered afterward would help us reconcile living a new life without her physical presence. On the airplane home, I reread the letter from Aaron's friend, Lynn Caruso, that quoted poet Mark Doty on how to live with the scar of loss.

And I thought of our own questions. How do we live with this crevasse in our lives? How do we weave her memory into the fabric of our family forever?

Lynn wrote,

> Doty describes the ancient Japanese ceramic cups. These cups were once the property of some holy monk, one of the few possessions he permitted himself to keep. Centuries later, the cup was dropped and broken, but even in this condition it was too beautiful to simply destroy. So it was repaired, not with glue, which wouldn't hold for centuries to come, but with a thin seam of gold solder repairing the break in what could never truly be repaired perfectly. The gold solder added a beauty to the cup, making part of it quite visible. . . .
>
> The metaphor offers the possibility to "honor the part of oneself that's irreparable—to fill the crack with gold means to give the break prominence, to let it shine. Wearing its history, the old cup with its gilt scars becomes, I imagine, a treasure of another sort, whole in its own fragmentation, more deeply itself, veined with the evidence of time."[2]

To me, this image made sense. The rich stories given to us those two weeks added to other cherished memories of Krista's life. They become part of the gold solder we all need to heal. As a writer, I resonated with Doty's use of a metaphor. But it was still impossible to imagine how life would unfold without Krista's nearness.

Chapter 7

SAVORING SOLITUDE

Sorrow is a solitary road.

— Isabel Allende, *Paula: A Memoir,* written after
the death of her twenty-five-year-old daughter

QUESTION: IS A DESIRE AND NEED FOR SOLITUDE A HEALTHY
RESPONSE IN GRIEF?

The amount of solitude I craved throughout the first year surprised me. But a longing for solitude can be trusted. Krista died in late spring, shortly after Jim and I finished teaching. This placed us in the fortunate situation of having a summer break before we needed to go back to work. This span of time, which allowed our meaningful travel in Bolivia, is highly unusual in America's typical work force. Almost 90 percent of companies have a bereavement benefit, yet typically they provide only three days paid leave.[1] Consequently, employees often must return to work within a week of a major family death, unless they have accrued sick or vacation leave. This inevitably demands extra effort on nurturing oneself, especially if one craves solitude like I did.

Other grieving parents have expressed a similar need for "alone" time, even while simultaneously wanting significant connections with a few close family and friends. Author Isabel Allende, in her memoir *The Sum of Our Days,* describes a bleak period nearly three years after her daughter Paula died. She still couldn't shake off her grief. "I didn't know then that the sadness is never entirely gone; it lives on forever just below the skin." Feeling a drought as a writer, she continues,

> I was as active as always and few people suspected my state of mind, but deep in my soul I was moaning. I developed a taste for solitude; I wanted only to be with my family; people bothered me, my friends were reduced to three or four. I was spent. . . . I needed silence, but it became more and more difficult to find. . . . My sadness manifested itself in sleepless nights, dark clothing, the wish to live in a hermit's cave, and an absence of inspiration.[2]

As Allende knew, much-needed silence is very hard to come by in our culture.

Distinctions are often made between solitude and loneliness, even though they may look similar on the surface. Some psychologists consider solitude *the state of being alone without being lonely*, a positive and constructive state of engagement with oneself. This gives time for reflection, inner searching, growth, or enjoyment of some kind. Deep reading requires solitude, which also enhances thinking and creativity. Healthy solitude is something we cultivate, a time from which we draw refreshing sustenance, providing an opportunity to replenish ourselves.

"I was as active as always and few people suspected my state of mind, but deep in my soul I was moaning. I developed a taste for solitude. . . . I was spent. . . . I needed silence, but it became more and more difficult to find."
—*Isabel Allende*

In contrast, loneliness is often considered a harsh punishment, a deficiency state, a state of discontent marked by a sense of estrangement, an awareness of excess aloneness. Solitude is something you choose. Loneliness often feels imposed on you by others. For some, seeking solitude in grief can be a healing choice, even if one also feels deep loneliness caused by loss.

Temperamentally, we all vary in the amount of solitude we need. Some solitude seems essential, giving us a chance to gain perspective, renewing us for the responsibilities of life. But what is needed and healthy for one person might create depression for another, especially if loneliness depletes them. As prisons know, solitary confinement is the ultimate harsh punishment.

When classes began in September, grief still felt so strong that I requested a one-course reduction in teaching. Then I had to teach only in the mornings. Often, working alongside the energy and vibrancy of college students seemed helpful. Yet, it also felt like I wrapped a "professional wall" around me. This allowed me to do my job without transferring such pain to students. But certain days, such as near Krista's birthday or the anniversary of her death, I found it hard to teach. On Krista's birthday, a student brought a small birch Celtic harp into my office and played "It's a Gift to Be Simple." We sang this Quaker song at Krista's memorial services, and hearing the magical sounds of the folk harp gave comfort. Sometimes, something triggered the raw sorrow. Then I'd find myself in Pamela Parker's faculty office, a good friend and colleague. I could cry with her for a few minutes before facing a classroom of students again.

In my first week back, students in my freshman writing class read Isak Dinesen's brief description of shooting an iguana from her book *Out of Africa*. She vividly describes her attraction to the brilliant shimmering hues of the Iguana scales, and her choice to shoot one to bring it home. Her use of concrete details demonstrates to students the power of language. We started to read the first part:

> I have sometimes come upon the Iguana, the big lizard, as they were sunning themselves upon a flat stone in a river-bed. They are not pretty in shape, but nothing can be imagined more beautiful than their coloring. They shine like a heap of precious stones or like a pane cut out of an old church window. When, as you approach, they swish away, there is a flash of azure, green and purple over the stones, the color like a comet's luminous tail.
>
> Once I shot an Iguana. I thought that I should be able to make some pretty things from his skin. A strange thing happened then, that I have never afterwards forgotten. As I went up to him, where he was lying dead upon his stone, and actually while I was walking the few steps, he faded and grew pale, all color died out of him as in one long sigh, and by the time that I touched him he was grey and dull like a lump of concrete. It was the live impetus blood pulsating within the animal, which had radiated out all that glow and splendor. Now that the flame was put out, and the soul had flown, the Iguana was as dead as a sandbag.[3]

While discussing how the exquisite colors drained out to a bland gray as the iguana died, I immediately flashed back to the worst day in my life. Krista's body had arrived from Bolivia to the Spokane funeral home, and Jim and I needed to see her to say good-bye. As I walked up to the open coffin and touched the rigid body and cold skin of our once luminous daughter, I wailed. Shocked by the icy truth of death, I collapsed to the floor. Reliving this harsh memory, and the visual loss of Krista's vibrant living splendor, I could barely finish teaching these unsuspecting students. After class, I fled home to be alone.

Could fear of further loss subtly keep a parent stuck and mired in memories, thus preventing a desire to engage in the world again?

"Grief is like an ocean beach," reflected a woman pastor as we shared coffee one day. "Waves come steadily for a while, and then suddenly a giant wave comes crashing in." Her description reminded me of the "rogue wave" that killed an unsuspecting science faculty colleague while he was beachcombing with his family on the wild coast of Oregon.

For months, I relished returning each afternoon to the stillness and sanctuary of our home. Earlier, friends asked me to tell of our encounters in Bolivia. "It's almost too powerful to talk about," I said. "But I'll write it." So, starting around 1 p.m., I sat in a wicker rocking chair and usually cried and wrote. Other times, I savored reading Krista's e-mails to us and her friends, or rereading her journals. Or, I'd sit and do nothing. What I remember most while attending to this deep sorrow was how close I felt to Krista. Although sorrowful, it was also a comforting time to be alone.

If and when such raw pain eased, would I also lose the tender closeness I felt toward Krista during these times of solitude? I began to wonder. Could fear of further loss subtly keep a parent stuck and mired in memories, thus preventing a desire to engage in the world again?

One friend expressed dismay over my retreat. "Why don't you just call me to come over when you feel sad?" But, perhaps because the mornings involved relating in positive ways to dozens of students and faculty, I really longed for time alone. I also limited companionship to a very close circle, people who didn't need me to talk all the time about what I was feeling. I could just be.

Other parents described how they sought to meet a similar desire for solitude. But they needed to find ways that proved feasible within the demands of their lives. When Jan Skaggs's twenty-year-old daughter Cameron died in March, it took months before Jan had any time to pause. "Within six weeks after her death, we had a lot of pre-planned commitments that we felt we needed to honor," recalls Jan. "Then, that fall my husband Harold, who was Cameron's close stepfather, was diagnosed with prostate cancer. We became immersed in the decision-making process for medical treatments." At the end of several months, a friend who had also endured major grief saw Jan. Alarmed at her condition as Jan coped with facing the potential of another loss, her friend insisted, "You need solitude." Jan's husband was going into treatment in Houston, so he found her a small beach cottage in Galveston to rent. "It was a pivotal five days for me. I hardly knew how to have solitude," admits Jan. "But a skilled counselor suggested several practical things."

"Mothers get grieving rights forever; fathers less so because they seem to feel this need to be strong for others. Stepfathers are even lower on the rung, yet they have often been quite close to a child."
—*Jan Skaggs*

He told Jan to bring the Bible and only one book, drink lots of water, get gross motor exercise, and bring something creative to do. "He wanted me to access both the right and left side of my brain." During stress, the counselor found that people often drink far more coffee and alcohol than water. He advised to fix simple meals, eat when you are hungry, and sleep when you are tired. Jan chose to bring the book *Song of the Seed: A Monastic Way of Tending the Soul*. For the first three days, she felt like she was stripped of false ideas and preconceptions, especially relating to her image of God.

> I had a rather formulaic concept of God, sort of like if I do A, B, and C, then God will, of course, do X, Y, and Z. So since I had tried to live a Christian life, with prayer, church attendance, and raising Cameron to be immersed in scripture and faith (my ABC), then I assumed God was obliged to protect and provide for us (my XYZ). But, really, my unstated assumption was I expected God to answer prayers the way I wanted.
>
> Then I felt like I encountered the holiness and sovereignty of God. God is not an idea, nor under my control. Cameron's death became part of a far bigger picture, a much larger sense of God, a mystery.

This experience, which she called both thrilling and terrifying, has left Jan with a lasting sense of awe and peace. One definition of contemplation is "to create space for the divine to enter," and Jan believed she experienced this rich possibility.

She also became more acutely aware of how her husband was affected by his stepdaughter's death. Cameron was a child he raised with patient commitment even when she first rejected him. They eventually became quite close when Cameron trusted he was in her life to stay. One of his last cherished memories occurred when Cameron returned home from college. "She wandered into my office, affectionately rubbed my balding head, and then climbed up into my lap and just snuggled closely," recalls Harold. "No words, just an impulsive gesture of trusting love."

"Mothers get grieving rights forever; fathers less so because they seem to feel this need to be strong for others. Stepfathers are even lower on the rung, yet they have often been quite close to a child," believes Jan. "We have a friend who lost a son who now reads obituaries. When he sees a child has died, he calls the father out of the blue six weeks later and invites him for a cup of coffee to talk about his grief."

Busy parents expressed ways they created small moments of solitude in their days or week. Rev. John Perkins was shattered by the death of his middle-aged son, a leader committed to continuing Perkins's ministry with the poor in Mississippi. In the early months, his weekly walk to the cemetery gave him a pattern of exercise and attention to grief. "I'd go to the gravesite alone every Saturday morning and on holidays. It's about a mile away, and it gave me exercise and therapy. I'd talk to him, bring fresh flowers, and spend five or ten minutes there. It was a healing time I could count on."

Babs Egolf began attending Eastern Washington University after the death of her teenage son. She discovered a water tower on campus that faced the Palouse, a beautiful agricultural area in eastern Washington state. She started going there whenever she needed release from seeing young people near the age of her son. "I would sit and write in my journal, sometimes do tai chi, write out my feelings, or just cry. It clearly wasn't appropriate to be crying in the classroom. Then I could go back."

She also found that the silent retreats sponsored by Hospice offered enormous solace. "I learned to practice meditation and became far more connected to my emotions and thoughts during these week-long retreats with strangers," said Babs. "At first, I sat next to the door with the EXIT sign so I could flee if I felt like it. But the sense of compassion and acceptance of suffering and pain as a familiar place helped. I learned to sit with the pain. It was a safe environment to do personal work." By meeting others facing loss, she gained understanding on how grief comes in many ways, whether caused by illness, a divorce, or death.

One mother couldn't face entering her seventeen-year-old daughter's room after a tragic car accident. A friend came over and refreshed the room by stripping the bed, hanging up clothes, clearing the chaos of a busy teenager's life. Then the mother found her daughter's bedroom actually a place of peaceful retreat. She would go in and sit on her daughter's bed for hours, often reading her journal left on the desk.

After her second-born son, Chris, died during an icy accident in Chicago, Sheree Capulli felt a vast need for privacy. A mother of five children, Sheree basically hibernated in her house for almost a year. She put his pictures up on the living room mantle with candles. After getting the other four kids off to school, she shut the blinds and grieved. She also found herself talking to him. "I just considered him to be living on a different plane. I felt his encouragement to 'be the best we can be.' It's what he would want from all of us."

Normally a fun-loving mother with a deep Christian faith, her need to withdraw kept her isolated. "I didn't go to the kids hockey games, avoided the grocery store, and any parties. I knew people stared at me—the mother whose son was killed." She found the second half of that first year harder than the first, especially as she came up to the anniversary of his death. Finally she agreed to go to a bunko group in the neighborhood. But a near stranger asked her too many private questions, and she resented the intrusion. "I also felt I had no business laughing. How could I have fun when my son is in the cemetery?"

Sheree also faithfully kept a journal during this first year. After a year, a breakthrough came when she returned to the grocery store. A friend saw her and said, "Oh Sheree, I miss seeing you. I'm afraid we'll never have Sheree back . . . our funny Sheree." This began her reengagement with others as her desire for solitude eased. "I recognized that my love meant something to others, and that my former joy in life was valued."

"I was overwhelmed by people," recalls Lila Girvin, after Matthew died in a UNICEF helicopter accident in Mongolia. During the next six months, she wanted very little social contact except with the closest of friends and family. "He was so companionable and we were so close. Even while abroad, we e-mailed almost daily. His three brothers and my husband and I all held him in wonder at the choices in his life, and his great love for the world's children."

She did not go back to the studio right away. But she had committed to an upcoming show, and friends and family urged her to paint in the midst of her pain. "They shoved me out the door," she recalls. To her amazement, luminous light filled the large canvases that emerged in the next months, not the pain she felt. These hours alone became a healing time. "I've always considered myself a spiritual searcher, reading and looking for what it means to live a full life. Teachings that called one back from the past or into the future were my constant companions. But painting always anchored me in the "now."

When friends give a grieving person a
sense of patience, recognizing that profound
loss takes enormous time and energy,
grievers are immensely grateful.

Lila sought professional counseling just one time because she found that meeting with other bereaved mothers and fathers far more helpful. A poem from Denise Lassaw that explores the transformative experiences of grief and the impermanence of life became especially meaningful for her. Lassaw wrote this in the midst of grieving the death of her thirty-eight-year-old husband, Ngodup Paljor, a former monk who fled from Tibet with the Dalai Lama. Killed suddenly while working on the Anchorage docks as a longshoreman, this Sanskrit scholar talked with his wife often about the Buddhist concept of impermanence.

Impermanence

I am being
cut with the Diamond Sword.
The pain of this wound
tears away all illusions
but wouldn't kill me.
Nor can I refuse to suffer

I, who CELEBRATED
every color and form,
who welcomed EVERYTHING
like a galaxy expanding
in delight.

I STAMP MY FOOT
I STAMP MY FOOT
AND HOWL![4]

As an artist, Lila resonated with Lassaw's words. "There is no way of making sense of a loss like this."

When Lila began to venture back into the community, her primary choice of place was a small local library. "It was the only place I could go alone," she remembers, appreciative that she could find solitude in a public place. "I wandered around the stacks, looking for books that might be helpful in poetry, the arts, and philosophy. I was so grateful that no one bothered me." Looking for authors who might give light to her broken heart became her first step back into the community.

When friends give a grieving person a sense of patience, recognizing that profound loss takes enormous time and energy, grievers are immensely grateful. During these long months of mourning, one close friend, Pamela Parker, sent me thoughtful notes. These often included relevant poetry. She gave me a wonderful sense that it was OK to take all the time I needed alone but that she was alongside me in spirit.

Since we both found joy in gardening and nature, she knew I'd likely love the Irish poet-priest, John O'Donohue.

"Beannacht"

On the day when
the weight deadens
on your shoulders
and you stumble,
may the clay dance
to balance you.

And when your eyes
freeze behind
the grey window
and the ghost of loss
gets in to you,
may a flock of colours,
indigo, red, green,
and azure blue
come to awaken in you
a meadow of delight.

When the canvas frays
in the currach of your thought
and a stain of ocean
blackens beneath you,
may there come across the waters
a path of yellow moonlight
to bring you safely home.

May the nourishment of the earth be yours,
may the clarity of the light be yours,
may the fluency of the ocean be yours,
may the protection of the ancestors be yours.

And so may a slow
wind work these words
of love around you,
an invisible cloak
to mind your life.[5]

During the first year, when I sought solitude, my husband found himself in an opposite trajectory, immersing himself into responsibilities and leadership at Whitworth University and at First Presbyterian Church. I sensed he felt a need to stay strong and keep the pain at bay because I was in such visible distress. Instead, during the first year, he seemed to grab "snatches" of solitude. Music affected him profoundly. I'd often see him fighting tears during hymns in church. Although we always loved "Be Thou My Vision," which was sung at our wedding, I doubt either of us noticed the words in the last stanza until Krista died. "Christ of my own heart, *whatever befall*, still be my vision, O Ruler of all." Now he'd just hold my hand tighter as we sang this.

"At times I felt emotionally dead, like I had flatlined. I so missed her joy in our family life, and I didn't find the joy and laughter in normal life routines like before. My fear was I'd be flat forever."
—Jim Hunt

At night, he'd find comfort listening to Eric Clapton's album *Pilgrim,* which was written after the death of Clapton's four-year-old son Conor. Clapton described it as "his saddest album" and included songs such as "My Father's Eyes," "River of Tears," and "Broken Hearted." In the stillness and privacy of our living room, Jim could face the multitude of memories of Krista. He especially treasured his memories as a father introducing her to Central America, a land he loved. While a college sophomore, Krista left the University of Puget Sound to join Whitworth's Central America study/service semester where her dad was a faculty leader. During these late evenings, he let himself feel his desolation.

"At times I felt emotionally dead, like I had flatlined. I so missed her joy in our family life, and I didn't find the joy and laughter in normal life routines like before. My fear was I'd be flat forever. I operated more out of duty, putting one step ahead of the other." He also began adding bird feeders to the garden and found solace watching the delightful bird life that ensued.

One evening, when Jim was outside by the stairway to Krista's memorial garden, I called him in for dinner. Unlike him, he just stayed outside, lost in an evening of grief. Later that night he penned this poem.

A Season of Death

Cold, skeleton-like limbs spiked the darkness.
Jet black skies enveloped dim walkway lights.
This is the season of death.

Crispy, prostrate brown leaves and twigs
rustle across a cement patio.
Somber, dusky freshets plunge downward
into an inky pool with soaked leaves.

Stairs arch upwards to the inscribed stone,
"Krista, A Joy Forever."
Her ashes strewn underneath chrysanthemums
and a Weeping Cherry.
And I weep too. Desolation is so vast.

It's been six months since that bright spring morn
turned storm grey and rainy
with arched rainbow pierced by lightning
brought a huge hole in my heart.
I walk the season of death and embrace it:

The stick skeletons, the inky pool, the vast darkness
and a measured walk to the stone.
Her stone; beloved, even in death. I weep.

Couples often mention the differences in how they each grieved their loss. With the added reality of divorces, blended families, stepparents, and absent parents, there are often multiple layers to a family's dynamic. Some consider these differences predictable by gender. Women are typically described as more emotional; men hold their emotions within. Men hold more anger; women cry with more guilt. Using a different lens, Kenneth Doka, coauthor of *Grieving Beyond Gender: Understanding the Ways Men and Women Mourn*, identifies two distinct grieving styles.[6] These are commonly associated, but not restricted, to gender. His interest and observations began thirty-nine years ago as a pediatric chaplain at Memorial Sloan-Kettering Cancer hospital.

Couples often mention the differences in how they each grieved their loss.

He believes men tend to grieve in an "instrumental" style; they prefer actions, working through the pain by doing and thinking. He illustrates this with the example of a bereft father, on the morning of his daughter's funeral, fixing the picket fence through which his daughter crashed. In our local community, John Baker found concrete actions life-giving after his daughter Krista died in 2000 of cystic fibrosis while waiting for a lung transplant. He has made it a decade-long quest to honor his daughter by raising awareness of the need for donor organs. Often he speaks in our local high school assemblies to urge teenagers to become designated donors when they get their driver's license. He finds that statistics bore students, even hearing that there are 110,000 people in the United States in need of organ and tissue transplants, and that eighteen die each day waiting. "But the minute I show them a photo of a beautiful young woman, and say I want them to know about my daughter Krista Lynn Baker who suffered from a dreadful disease before lungs became available, their yawning stops." Once she was listed on the transplant list, his daughter's hopes soared. "Everywhere we went, she carried her beeper hoping for a call. She was down to 100 pounds, still clutching her beeper, but the call never came."[7] His hope is her story will save some lives.

Brendan Wiechert understands. When he lost his forty-year-old beloved sister Megan Alden, who left two young daughters behind, he knew his own children also grieved the loss of their fun-loving, energetic aunt. So he built an elaborate tree house for all the children, including a trapdoor, zip line, and fire pole exit. A plaque affixed to the base of the tree dedicates it to Megan,

> whose enthusiasm and joy in new adventures opened a door to the wonders of this world. May this place perpetuate her spirit, inspire our imaginations, and make us laugh.

He then built a suspension bridge connecting two platforms with seventeen planks. He inscribed each plank with favorite quotes from poems, books, and films like the *Calvin and Hobbes* quote, "It's a magical world, Hobbes, ol'buddy . . . let's go exploring." His hope is that the children will be able to come here and remember their mother and aunt without it feeling like they were going to a cemetery. "Building it was very therapeutic for him," said his wife, Debbie.[8]

Doka observes that women are typically "intuitive" grievers, more feeling-oriented, with waves of emotion and much verbalizing. They often find ways to express feelings in a group, or with a therapist or confident. Two years after her fifteen-year-old daughter was murdered in a killing of six teenagers at a party in Seattle, Nancie Thorne describes her initial attempts to push back the grief, to somehow escape the suffocating pain and despair she felt. Eventually she realized this was impossible. "It can't be done, though. You can't get away from it. You have to accept it." What proved pivotal, after floundering for months, was the help she found through a community of Seattle-area counselors and therapists. Instead, they taught her how to embrace the suffering. So grateful for such guidance and the peace that was emerging, she helped initiate a free event in the city called "Changing the Face of

Grief." All who are suffering loss in isolation are invited to receive similar help. Nancie recognized that "many don't have resources or know how to get the help they need, to connect with people who know what they are going through."[9] It's her firm conviction that one cannot possibly "go it alone" after sudden traumatic loss.

Although these general patterns may prevail, Doka cautions that these styles are not restricted to gender. Some women may primarily express grief through actions; some men may find comfort in sharing their hurt. However, because grief counselors historically have privileged expression, men or women who work out pain "instrumentally" often wonder if they are "grieving" enough. Other family members may also express frustration over someone's lack of emotional expression over loss. These judgments hurt everyone. My sense is our ways of living with grief also vary simply by one's temperament and the relationship with the child. Instead, I value Isabel Allende's words that say "sorrow is a solitary road."

Solitude opens a way to navigate this journey. Jim also lost his father shortly after Krista's death, but it wasn't until his sabbatical that he felt he could absorb his own enormous pain. He sought solitude through a solo backpacking trip in the Hoh River Valley on Washington's Olympic Peninsula, one of Krista's favorite places. For hours, he hiked trails in the soothing rainforest mist of September's sun and shadows with Scout, our flat-back retriever. He came home more acutely in touch with all he'd lost as a father and son, but clearly he was refreshed in spirit.

As Jim and I walked together in this new land of loss, we both withdrew into solitude at times. My trust and hope was that the reservoir and resilience of almost thirty years of living and loving together offered a protective holding space as we each traveled down this solitary road.

Chapter 8

SEEKING COMPANIONS
ALONG THE WAY

You need not walk alone.

—The mission of Compassionate Friends,
an organization for bereaved families.

cx/xp

QUESTION: IN WHAT WAYS IS COMPANIONSHIP ESSENTIAL IN A
GRIEF JOURNEY?

Off the Northumberland coast of England lies Lindisfarne, one of the Sea Islands that is linked to the mainland only by a causeway. Twice a day the tide covers the causeway. Some consider this sacred place, also known as the Holy Island, as the cradle of Christianity where a monastery was founded in 634 AD. Here monks produced the famous illuminated manuscript known as the Lindisfarne Gospel, which now resides in the British Museum. Abandoned during the Viking raids and dormant for years, Lindisfarne has now become a center for the revival of Celtic Christianity and a popular retreat destination. When the tide recedes, the island abounds with activity as thousands of tourists arrive. However, most visitors leave before the tide returns and cuts them off. After the onslaught of daily tourism, once again it becomes a much quieter place for those two hundred permanent residents who stay.

A companion with a good listening ear can be like a life raft in the shifting tide of sorrow.

Each day the island community experiences this swinging of the pendulum from sharing to solitude. Although many persons in grief appreciate some solitude, almost all say sharing companionship and community are essential too. The phrase "to grieve" means "to bear a heavy burden," and we need others to walk with us to help carry this load. In the early months, this need to move between solitude and community often abounds. Only we don't have a physical sea tide to mark these moments of shifting change.

In a similar vein, grief counselors make a distinction between shifting from private grief to public mourning. Grief is seen as *internal*, the constellation of thoughts and feelings we have when someone we love dies. We can think of grief as a container that holds all our thoughts and feelings and images of our experiences when we are bereaved, and the meaning we give to this experience of loss. In our culture, too often people believe they are to "keep grief to yourself."

In contrast, mourning is *external*. We take the grief that is inside and express it outside of ourselves. The ritual of a public funeral or memorial service, expressing our hearts and minds through art, music, or writing; celebrating anniversaries; or simply crying and talking about the one we've loved and lost are all expressions of mourning. To mourn is to heal. A companion with a good listening ear can be like a life raft in the shifting tide of sorrow.

Native American cultures recognize the necessity of consciously grieving and mourning. Different tribal cultures create vessels, baskets, pots, or bowls, all symbols to contain one's grief. They can be put away and then brought out regularly to mourn.

It is similar to counselor's advice to "dose" ourselves with grief little by little; breaks in between are essential. The hope in facing and sharing grief, gently and in small doses, is that this death can be reconciled so that one can grow in trust that life can be good again. Engaging in the work of mourning with companions along the way often proves pivotal.

Every person I've ever spoken with who has lost someone they love expresses a kind of eternal gratefulness for some particular kindnesses they experienced in the immediate days after a death. John Perkins, a prominent civil rights leader and pastor, was sixty-nine when he lost his firstborn son to a sudden heart attack. He recalls the importance of others during those first moments and days:

> They called me to the hospital and the shock of seeing my large son laying there . . . he's a big guy and had died on the table. I felt a desperation. He's still my baby and needing me so desperately, and there was nothing I could do. . . .

He'd always seen me as a "take charge" father. This continued during the civil rights battles in the South even after visiting me in jail where I'd been severely beaten and was extremely vulnerable from police brutality. I have a vague memory that meant so much to me. A chaplain came to the hospital and just put his hand on my shoulder without saying a word. It was his presence that meant everything.

Perkins recalls other thoughtful gestures from their community that gave his wife and him solace. "We would wake up and hear congregational members in the house, washing dishes, fixing breakfast, day and night . . . it was so comforting. I couldn't imagine facing this sorrow of losing Spencer without them. I still swell up with gratitude remembering peoples gripping loving presence." Later, an artist friend drew a smiling portrait of his dynamic son, a rising young leader in their small town." It stimulates me and reminds me of his presence . . . it's a beautiful painting."

When Isador Duncan, a dancer, lost two young children in a drowning accident in the Seine River, she found refuge with actress Eleanora Duse in Italy in 1913. Frustrated that most of her companions tried to cheer her up, instead Eleanora fully embraced her and consoled her pain. "When Eleanora said, 'Tell me about Deirdre and Patrick,' and made me repeat to her all their little sayings and ways, and show her their photos, she kissed and cried over them. She never said, 'Cease to grieve,' but she grieved with me, and for the first time since their death, I felt I was not alone."[1]

As Duncan first experienced, finding companionship isn't always easy. For some, family and close friends or neighbors offer open friendship. But not always. Many parents found their closest community came through new friendships with other parents who encountered a similar shock and loss. "The Candlelighters group meant everything to me after Larry died," said Barbara Grigsby, who poured her broken heart into helping other parents going through grief. This organization (now called ACCO, American Childhood Cancer Organization), which works specifically for children undergoing cancer treatment, became a lifeline. "The hospital sponsored events during the years our son was being treated, so we met other parents going through similar pain and fear. We could tell our stories, cry together, and support each other." After her son died, she especially appreciated the impromptu times of friendship that continued. "We usually met for lunch once a month, but lots of other times came up to do things together which proved very comforting. We understood each other."

Another group many parents have found invaluable is Compassionate Friends, begun by a chaplain in England forty years ago. He brought two grieving families together and saw that the support they gave each other surpassed anything he could say or provide. Since then it has crossed the ocean to America, and there are over 625 chapters throughout the country and in thirty other nations. They assist parents, siblings, and grandparents who lose a child at any age to enter into healthy and natural grieving. Their intent is to help transform the pain and isolation of grief into healing and hope. Anyone who calls their phone number or contacts them on their Web site will find a community of care.

Similar groups are emerging for parents who lose a stillborn or newborn. The international MISS Foundation offers a virtual online community, conferences, plus seventy-five chapters around the world to provide support for all parents in bereavement. They also are pioneering education and legislative efforts to draw visibility to the estimated 2.6 million stillbirths a year, an international reality often neglected by the global public health community. With 7,300 babies born dead each day, just as a family expects to welcome a new life, the devastation is immense.

How mothers are treated during such profound loss is changing, hospital by hospital. At Sacred Heart Children's Hospital in Spokane, their pioneering Forget-Me-Not program begun in 2006 is transforming the way parents and health-care professionals come alongside parents to help with this unique grief. "In ancient times, stillborn babies and those born with birth defects were considered evil omens, punishment by God for a parent's misdeeds," says Sarah Bain, whose daughter Grace died in her womb two days before she was born in 2003. She felt so bereaved with the lack of support and information she describes this as "the most isolating experience in my life."

"In modern times, mothers tend to blame themselves. Pregnant women all get the list. Don't drink, don't eat soft cheeses, eat organic. So you think, 'Was it that one day I threw up and didn't take my prenatal vitamins? If you don't have the support, it's easy to fall into the traps of blame and shame.'"[2] Now Sarah volunteers with the national Miss Foundation, in affiliation with the Forget-Me-Not hospital program to help other families not feel such aloneness. In contrast to earlier customs, in some hospitals parents are no longer rushed out after a baby dies. Extended family may hold the baby, volunteer photographers offer to take photographs, and plaster molds are made of feet and hands, whatever a family chooses if they want some remembrance.

Online communities have sprung up around very specific situations for child loss. SPALS (Subsequent Pregnancy after a Loss Support) became a source of solace for Meredith Banka during the years she suffered three miscarriages during her thirties, including the loss at twenty weeks of a little boy they named Gabriel. Working in a high-level corporate position, she didn't necessarily desire to talk with other professionals at work about the multiple surgeries and emotional roller coaster she was living. "SPALS was super helpful. I formed friendships with other women sharing similar questions around health issues, medical solutions, and our fears and hopes in future pregnancy." When Meredith and her husband, Chris, eventually adopted a little boy, her online friends rejoiced. Some even shared pictures on Facebook. Similar organizations exist for families who have lost a child through murder or suicide. For families not living near larger cities where local support chapters exist, the advent of various virtual communities provides another way that some parents break through their sense of isolation.

"In modern times, mothers tend to blame themselves. Pregnant women all get the list. Don't drink, don't eat soft cheeses, eat organic. . . . If you don't have the support, it's easy to fall into the traps of blame and shame."
—*Sarah Bain*

Mari Bailey also appreciates how research on the Internet can connect a grieving parent to others. I first heard Mari on a PBS broadcast in 2013 in a series "Losing Our Religion after Tragedy: Nonbelievers Find Other Ways to Cope." In subsequent conversations, she told me more of how her twenty-one-year-old son Michael returned home to Phoenix in 2004 after a tour in the Navy where he served as a submarine cook. While visiting a friend one evening, an acquaintance also dropped by. He started yelling and waving a gun, and then shot Michael at close range, leading to his violent death.

"I was beside myself with grief," recalls Mari, "and thought I was losing my soul." Raised in the church, seeking solace in religion was "second nature" to Mari. She was confirmed in the church as a child, attended a Catholic grade school and an all-girl Catholic high school. As she became busier in adulthood, raising children as a single parent, teaching full time, and going to college, she found herself not as consistent in attending their large parish church. "But when Michael was murdered, my first instinct was to visit a priest for solace and some perspective."

However, her experience proved disheartening. "I could tell from the priest's body language that he was really uncomfortable with my grief. Because of the turnover in church leadership, we didn't know each other. Then he started giving me spiritual platitudes like "God doesn't give you more than you can handle," "this is your cross to bear," and "God has a reason for everything that happens." When he said to me, "'It was God's time to call Michael home, and he is in a better place,' I wanted to scream and say, 'Being at home with his Mom and hanging out with his friends is a better place.' I needed solace and comfort, not someone to try to defend God."

At first, she just tried praying on her own. But then Mari found herself really angry. "I wondered, why do I have to pray for strength? Why was my child killed . . . six others were in the room and only Michael was shot. What kind of a God allows someone's child to be shot?"

This proved a turning point for Mari. "I've never felt so alone . . . with a sense that God was not here to help me. I was done with the church and with God. It was pivotal. I felt I was now on my own; I had to save myself."

In desperation, she began intensive research in the library trying to educate herself on traumatic death and bereavement. "I had no frame of reference before Michael's murder. I didn't know how I was supposed to act or what I was supposed to do." A few weeks later, Mari typed into an Internet search engine, "my child was killed and I feel like I'm going crazy." The organization Parents of Murdered Children came up in the search, and there was even a local chapter in Phoenix. "I was scared to go to the first meeting, but I immediately found a community of other parents who understood what I was going through. We've all been traumatized, some with far more brutal circumstances. I don't have to worry that if I want to talk about Michael that the members will feel like, 'Oh crap, she's going to talk about her dead child again.'"

Not only did Mari find companions, the community has provided a place for her to help other parents as one of their local monthly leaders. "I find my greatest healing comes when I serve others." Mari's informal research eventually led to writing her graduate school dissertation on the topic of grief. Mari currently serves on the Board of Directors for Parents of Murdered Children. In addition, Mari speaks at various bereavement conferences.

Our own large church, like many others, offers support groups for those experiencing bereavement of any kind. For parents of a suicide, one of the most overwhelming child deaths, community often proves absolutely pivotal. Steve Nelson, whose twenty-year-old son Carl took his life during a time of college stress, suffered silently during his initial shock. Later, he found this church grief group immensely valuable, particularly the journal exercises. "I was uncomfortable with some of the assignments at first," he admits. "I heard others in the class say, 'I feel worse now than when I started.' And it was true! But it was also a sign that we were working through some very hard stuff . . . and it was well worth it."

In one of his journal entries Steve wrote a letter to his son, Carl, who had helped him build a new addition to their home. Part of the letter included:

Dear Carl,

I was inside our new addition, working on the house, or at least trying to. But my mind kept drifting, and I kept thinking about you. I moved a box of nails on my workbench and found your brown leather tool belt lying neatly underneath. I picked it up and unfolded it, gently extending the belt to its full width. You'd worn this tool belt a few months ago while stapling house wrap around the outside of our new addition. It was the last job we worked on together before you packed up your clothes, climbed into your Honda and drove away to Seattle. Your blue eyes were full of promise and light. You had high expectations about things to come. You knew your math and physics classes would be tough, but you showed such a strong mind and were filled with quiet confidence. We all knew you would succeed, no matter what the professors asked you to do.

I carefully unfolded the tool belt, looking for something inside. Anything. I'm not sure why. Inside the worn leather pouch I found an assortment of nails, screws, and drywall dust leftover from jobs that you and I worked on last summer. This tool belt almost felt like holy ground. I picked up a nail from the pocket. You had held this nail in your fingers only a few months ago.

In recent days I've continued to work on the house. . . . But each time, at some point in the day, I stop my work, I set down my tools, and I drop my head in despair. Each time my eyes fill with tears, and my heart cries out. An overwhelming sense of grief fills my soul, and it's like I can't even hear anything outside of me. I cry until my face hurts. I'm surrounded by reminders of you. And there is no joy in them. You aren't coming back. Not to work. Not to visit. Not to even say goodbye.

He found being able to imagine talking to his son and then doing another journal entry with his son's imagined response "opened my eyes to what I have been feeling." He also appreciated the counsel to "throw away the stop watch" and expectations that he will "get over" grief.

Gloria Nielsen, a former hospital chaplain who has led First Presbyterian Church of Spokane grief groups for over ten years, discovered several universal experiences happen when communities gather intentionally around loss and bereavement. "Many say that listening to others normalizes grief . . . they realize they aren't going crazy. Being with others who listen and accept you as you are provides an anchor. No one is trying to fix you and urging 'are you back to normal yet?'"

She believes that grief shared is grief halved. If a person can identify their feelings, they can begin the process of gaining peace within themselves. One woman, who lost an infant at two days old over forty years ago, came to deal with much that had been suppressed. "I still had a lot of hidden pain. It has been very helpful to revisit that part of my life. To take the time so many years later to remember, and forgive, and let go of the pain of such an abrupt loss finally gave me a measure of peace. I also learned to allow myself to talk about Amy without feeling that people would think that I should be done with that by now." She also gained insight on who to share with in the future. "The class made me see that not every friend is up to hearing about your grief."

She believes that grief shared is grief halved.
—*Gloria Nielsen*

"How true," agrees Shelly Fry, who also attended Nielsen's class with her husband for three ten-week sessions after their twenty-five-year-old son Spencer (nicknamed Bear) died in 2010. "The classes were a lifeline for us." Bear was joyriding with a friend who drove a BMW at 100 miles-an-hour down a hill and hit a tree, killing all three men in the car. "It was such a senseless, unnecessary, stupid death," laments Fry, the mother of four sons. She felt particular agony since Bear had finally been in recovery from severe health and addiction challenges that lasted years.

Seven years earlier, while attending community college, their once healthy son awoke one morning with immense pain in his face. Over the years, the family visited over twenty-three doctors and specialists and endured several surgeries as they saw him become increasingly disabled, living with chronic pain. "Mom, you have to help me," he'd cry, and Fry gave her heart and soul and finances to find a diagnosis and relief.

A professional working woman, she became the one over the years taking time to seek medical assistance, travel, and care for him after complex surgeries. These absences jeopardized her employment situation that the family needed for medical expenses, a further stress. Eventually he was diagnosed with Neuralgia Trigeminal, and surgeries at the Mayo Clinic began to give him some relief. Then he relapsed after a massive seizure.

"Ours is a complicated grief and it is still raw.
I always looked forward to Tuesday nights for
our meetings, and bonded with some wonderful
friends. It was the best thing we ever did."

—*Shelly Fry*

"The pain is so intense they call it the suicide disease. I actually wouldn't have been so surprised if he had finally reached the end of his endurance," said Fry. "Our family has been active in a Presbyterian church since he was a child, and friends would come up to him during the years and say, 'We're praying for you.' He always thanked them, but as he said to me, 'Why bother? It obviously hasn't helped.' I know he felt in his heart that God let him down." Eventually the pain led to his self-medicating with an overuse of oxycotin, which he'd buy on the street to supplement his prescriptions. Then he augmented this with heroin. But shortly before the accident Bear had checked himself into rehab. "We were hopeful," said Fry.

"I was numb at first after his death, but then I found myself very angry. Why did God let this happen to someone who had endured so much already? If God had a perfect plan, how could this happen?" Her husband, who experienced comfort through Scripture and prayer, didn't share this anger. "I didn't feel his permission to be angry at God, but I explained that we can love someone deeply and be mad at the same time. It's almost embarrassing because I wish I could find the peace he has. I worry that our son was running in the fast lane, obviously not living a life that God would want." But the grief group has helped her be honest and patient with herself. "Ours is a complicated grief," she recognizes, "and it is still raw. I always looked forward to Tuesday nights for our meetings, and bonded with some wonderful friends. It was the best thing we ever did." She continues to meet once a month with friends she met during these earlier sessions.

When Barbara Hofmaier and David Heim received a call that Matthew, their firstborn son and a senior in college, had committed suicide, "our world turned upside down." Unlike suicides that are preceded by earlier bouts of mental illness or anguish, Matt had usually been upbeat. An avid athlete and sports fan, he loved being with people. His younger brother admired him greatly for his sociability and spirit of adventure. "Matt was really funny, a great storyteller who made times around the dining room table always fun," recalls Barbara. "He also enjoyed being with people of all ages—little kids and older people—at the tennis club where he worked." Matt majored in communications at Denison University in Ohio and was planning to pursue a career in sports broadcasting. "It's been heartbreaking," Barbara said four years later. "We had to rebuild our own lives and of course our self-esteem as parents. We thought we'd made good choices in our life for our children."

It was their deep community network that provided essential comfort. "What was really helpful was that our friends and faith community offered tremendous support . . . without any judgment. They seemed to recognize that all young people in our culture are very vulnerable." They also found the organization LOSS (Loving Outreach to Survivors of Suicide), which supports those left after a suicide.

It was eye-opening to hear the stories of others affected by the suicide of a loved one. Not everyone receives the kind of support from friends, family members, and a church congregation that we did.

We also recognized that we had a choice to make here . . . whether to keep hope alive. We were at a crossroads. Sometimes we received small significant gifts that lifted our spirits, like the day a friend of Matt's from years earlier came by and told us about a reunion where he and Matt had played a few rounds of golf together. He told us how much he loved and missed Matt.

Even finding one other mom or dad who has experienced such loss often provides priceless companionship. "The first counselor I visited mentioned she had lost a dog," recalls Babs Egolf. "There was no way I felt she'd understand." After a year of suffering alone, she found a bereavement counselor with a Hospice program in a nearby town. "She was an unbelievable mentor. She'd lost a son too, was a deep listener, suggested several valuable books like *Full Catastrophe Living,* and introduced me to meditation. Because of her I attended my first silent meditation retreat. I was so raw, but felt held by a room of people who understood suffering and trauma. I felt so connected to others and no longer alone."

Knowing how pivotal friendship can be after losing a child, a family in our community places a picture of their son Sky Blu Charbonneau in our local paper on the anniversary of his death. A talented artist, musician, and student with a 4.0 g.p.a. with a bright future, he committed suicide at age fourteen during a down moment several years ago. At the end of their tribute in memory of him, they write, "If you lost a teen to suicide, know that it was an emotional mistake. If you write, we'll answer," Mark and Terri Charbonneau.[3] Then they give their e-mail address.

After Krista's death my mother gave us a gift to build a small pond and waterfall in the garden in time for a late sum-

mer wedding reception for Susan and Peter. We found ourselves spending hours out there, often with Aaron and other
close family friends, reminiscing with stories, drinking a glass
of ice tea or wine, or just sitting in silence. Watching the active
bird and plant life engaged us in the community of creation.
These moments of deep companionship eased our hearts.

Above a stone staircase we created a garden in Krista's
memory, centered by a weeping cherry tree. A stone mason
carved the words *Krista Hunt Ausland, A Joy Forever* on a natural
granite rock. That fall, friends gathered with us to place some
of her ashes under a bed of chrysanthemums. Arching above
all of this is a sixty-year-old ailanthus tree, which we later
learned bears the common name "Tree of Heaven."

"We also recognized that we had a
choice to make here . . . whether to keep
hope alive. We were at a crossroads."
—*Barbara Hofmaier*

A robin built a nest in the cherry tree, giving us joy and
wonder as we saw the brilliant blue eggs and then watched the
antics of baby birds. For two summers, a hummingbird created
the tiniest of nests from spider webs on a Norway maple branch
near the pond, a source of endless fascination. During these
times, Jim felt solace and a sense of communion by watching
the cycles of life in nature. While feeding birds faithfully, he
loved seeing them build nests for their new families. "Life goes
on," he observed one night. "We're not such a big deal."

When we first moved to Spokane for Jim's teaching position
at Whitworth, I was a stay-at-home mom with young children.
Several other faculty families arrived that same year, and a group
of wives started a book club. We became such good friends that
the husbands decided they wanted to join the fun. This included
Don and Doris Liebert and Ron and Marianne Frase, the two

couples who came to our door that devastating May morning. For almost twenty-five years, we met once a month with several couples, though the nature of our gatherings evolved as our interests changed. Books simply became the conduit for rich life friendships. Together we shared the birth and adoption of children, re-entry into careers for each of the women, the trials and joys of raising teenagers, coping with serious illness, joy of nature and travel, and professional and personal passions. We always ended our times in prayer. Since most faculty members move to universities away from their families of origin, this community gave us a sense of kinship.

Don, Ron, and Jim developed a five-month Central America immersion study/service program for students, and they rotated their travel time abroad. Marianne and Doris, both very talented teachers, and I coauthored two books published by Herald Press to encourage children in healthy cooking and gardening with *Loaves and Fishes* and *Celebrate the Seasons*. Uncannily, Doris and I also received a breast cancer diagnosis around the same time in our fifties, as did Marianne later. With no siblings or parents nearby, we became surrogate family. They loved Krista like a niece, so they shared the shock and sorrow of our loss. "There was this huge numbness for weeks," recalls Doris. "All of us felt it." Don, a sociology professor who is also an ordained Presbyterian pastor, remembers at the end of the first traumatic day saying to Jim, "You'd think I'd be able to come up with some words of comfort."

> "Heart shattered lives . . . don't for
> a moment escape God's notice."
> —*Psalm 51* (The Message)

Jim responded, "So glad you didn't." We were all beyond words. For months, either Marianne or Doris telephoned daily, and we grieved together, remembering Krista.

Yet often words did console, especially cards that friends continued to send throughout the next years. One friend simply wrote out a contemporary version of a line in Psalm 51, a card I still keep near my desk. "Heart shattered lives . . . don't for a moment escape God's notice" (*The Message*).

My mother grew up as an only child, so it was my father's Norwegian family that gave us a sense of the community of aunts and uncles and cousins. A few years before Krista's death, Jim and I traveled to Norway on a research trip for my graduate studies. I came to explore the childhood of a Norwegian-American mother of nine who walked across America in 1896. Motivated by a $10,000 wager, she hoped to save their family farm when they couldn't pay the mortgage and taxes after the depression of 1893. While in Norway, we discovered my great grandfather's abandoned homestead near the beautiful Lofoten Islands.

My father died four months before Krista, and Mom decided after she'd lost her husband and Krista that she wanted to take our family on a reunion to Norway. What began as eight to ten family members grew to over twenty, including newlyweds Susan and Peter and our son Jefferson. Several cousins decided to bring their families along. This created a rare reunion since our families are spread so far apart across America. We rented little rorbuer cabins, once the old Norwegian cabins fisherman came to during storms. We enjoyed a wonderful week of fishing, midnight golf, laughter, shared meals, and meeting extended family in Norway. While visiting the twelfth-century stone church on the isle of Steigen where our ancestors once worshiped, we saw our family gravestones. We also traipsed on the old homestead land and met elderly neighbors who remembered my grandfather's family. All this fun and history gave Jim and me a sense of the ongoing strength of family even while simultaneously feeling this great emptiness without Krista. These treasured moments reminded us to be grateful and enjoy each person who is alive. Jim felt that a Northwest poet,

Theodore Roethke, expressed this beautifully in a line from his poem "The Far Field": *What I love is near at hand.*[4]

One of the clichés we heard from many people about the death of a child is "you are forever changed." I understand this much more now. However, at the time, we talked and agreed that there were some things we didn't want to change. For Jim, this included his commitment to continue to travel with students to Central America in the program he helped design with fellow professors and friends, Don and Ron. I supported his going, even knowing that he'd inevitably be riding buses on dangerous roads again. Whitworth University's immersion program introduces students to Honduras, Nicaragua, Guatemala, Mexico, El Salvador, and Costa Rica. It includes a month of living and working alongside a family, usually in the countryside, either in the fields, schools, or medical clinics. It gave Jim joy and meaning, seeing the transformation in students and faculty as they grew in understanding of our Latin American neighbors.

He also carried marvelous memories of being with Krista. In her sophomore year she withdrew from the University of Puget Sound to join her Dad on the semester-long program. A pre-med student at the time, faculty placed her in a Honduran medical clinic in an impoverished area of the coastal city of La Ceiba. Here she cleaned the wounds of battered women and saw her first HIV/AIDS slides under the microscope.

Krista bonded so closely with her new female friends on the study program that three of them later became her bridesmaids. When Jim returned to Central America to lead his six-week portion of the trip, two of Krista's bridesmaids now served as teaching assistants for the faculty. They also met up with two other friends of Krista's living and working in El Salvador and Nicaragua. Over meals together, Alycia Jones, Laurie Werner, Tracy King, and Julienne Gage reminisced with Jim. Struggling with their own sense of loss, they remembered times together juggling sticks on a Costa Rican plaza or enjoying Ecuadorian bands. They regaled him with previously untold stories about Krista and her college women friends dancing naked on a rooftop in Tegucigalpa to the rock music of the Violent Femmes. The friendship and laughter with these four close friends of Krista gave Jim unforgettable companionship in sorrow. "Grief shared is grief halved" became a living truth.

A sense of community also can come through new friends or even strangers. Jim loves to travel. His curiosity about the world gives him a sense of adventure whenever he enters a new land. Because he speaks workable Spanish, he enjoys any excuse to visit Central and South America. When he learned of an international conference on Service-Learning in Quito, Ecuador, he jumped at the invitation to present Whitworth University's life-shaping, five-month study/service-learning trip. He called one night sounding exceptionally upbeat. "They hold academic conferences so differently here," he marveled. "I love their joy." He described how they blended times of feasting, dancing, celebration, and friendships amid presenting academic papers. The conference and friendships he began became a turning point in rekindling his flagging spirits. In a candid moment, acknowledging how my deep sadness affected his own spirit, he admitted, "It's not like I come home to much joy in our home now." I appreciated that his tone wasn't judgmental, just a candid expression of our present reality. But it gave me pause.

After the conference, Jim hiked the trail into the sacred site of the Incas in Peru. For years he had studied and taught about Machu Picchu and was thrilled to finally be there. On the way back to Cusco he hopped on a bus. A Quechua Indian woman moved over to create an empty space for him to sit. An ample woman with a round face, wearing a print dress and knit sweater, she welcomed him with a warm, toothless smile. They began talking in Spanish, at first about the beauty of the day and mountains. Then the conversation took an unusual twist as they discovered they both had lost daughters. In silence, they shared this wonder. "I felt like it was a sacred encounter," Jim told me later. "Both daughters were twenty-five."

Jim wrote a poem of gratitude after this mysterious and wonder-filled encounter.

Quechua Dama

Hustled from train to bus
there, next to her, an empty seat.
She nodded approval of my occupying its emptiness.
Her stout frame amply filled the seat's corner.

I, long, white, and lank
appeared as if from a different world.
Brown hat, sunglasses, blue eyes, white skin.
She, dark, short, hair tinged with grey, teeth missing.
Still, she smiled and nodded.

We chatted in Spanish about
houses, trees, mountains, and families.
As the bus lurched along
our generalities became specifics.

I, a daughter died three years ago.
She, a daughter too in a bus accident.
Both, in magical ways were twenty-five.
Our eyes locked, both brimming with tears.
I choked mine back.

But she, lady that she was
dove deep into her blue plastic shopping bag
and lifted high a beautiful Peruvian pan.
She broke it and offered me some.[5]

Moments like this, which connected our loss of Krista into the universal loss of children from around the world, gave Jim much to ponder.

Chapter 9

ENCOURAGING CREATIVITY
TO EASE THE PAIN

*Creativity is a life force. The act of being creative connects us to
ourselves and something bigger than ourselves at the same time.*

—Ann Walker, Art Therapist, Providence Center
for Faith and Healing, Sacred Heart Medical Center

✿

QUESTION: WILL TANGIBLE CREATIVE ACTS HELP IN THE HEAL-
ING JOURNEY?

The loss of a loved one shatters not only our assumptions about life but often even our life routines and patterns. After a weekend gathering with a group of mothers who had lost children, someone mentioned, "Did you notice that almost every woman eventually stepped out of their familiar comfort zones and attempted something new?" It was true. Debilitating grief clearly has the power to constrict and narrow our life, closing us off from others and avoiding engaging in the world. But grief also propels many parents into creative actions, what researchers refer to as posttraumatic growth. These lead to new interests, friendships, even the development of skills and talents. "My heart is bigger since Etta's death," claims Pennye Nixon amazed at the direction her life has taken since starting Etta's Projects, which partners with Bolivian communities to address poverty. Whether learning how to quilt or cross-country ski, practicing the piano, traveling to a remote country, starting college classes in mid-life, embracing meditation, or creating a legacy in memory of their child, each door they enter has potential to expand a parent's world. And ease their pain.

Many nonprofits originate from families trying to create something meaningful that lifts above a tragedy. Some are major like Mothers Against Drunk Driving, Susan G. Komen Breast Cancer Awareness, or John Walsh's National Center for Missing or Exploited Children. But most are smaller, more modest endeavors, simply seeking a tangible way to honor their child.

"The Susie Forest," an innovative nonprofit in Spokane, began with the planting of three trees in 2003 by Nancy MacKerrow. She started this to remember Susie, her thirty-six-year-old daughter who was killed while walking in a crosswalk. Highly respected as a passionate activist, avid cyclist, environmentalist, and world traveler, Susie was committed to creating livable communities. "She had such joyful enthusiasm and optimism, she could pull people together to do good work, especially around bicyclist and pedestrian safety," said Nancy. Her idea for "Susie's

Trees" changed to "The Susie Forest" as Nancy found such satisfaction connecting with others as they added beauty to the environment. There are now over three hundred trees planted throughout Spokane and as far away as Iran, Brazil, Afghanistan, the Phillipines, Japan, Australia, and New Zealand. "Each tree is a reminder that life goes on and starts anew," said Nancy. Except on the anniversary of Susie's death and her birthday, all the other trees are in honor of others or organizations or historic events. "It's deeply personal . . . sometimes the birth of a baby, an anniversary, or the death of another child. But we've also planted in honor of the 100th anniversary of Women's Suffrage in Washington, for Boys and Girls Clubs, and schools."

When small nonprofits collaborate with other organizations, this enhances their impact. Nancy works closely with Reforest Spokane, a nonprofit organization within the city parks department. She particularly loves educating children on the gifts of shade, oxygen, and pollution reduction that trees give to urban environments. Equally meaningful are the rituals Nancy developed. Guests are invited to these public events, and Nancy provides each with a biodegradable "tree-gram." She invites people to write any messages, blessings, or prayers around the person or group being honored. After guests hang these from tree limbs, Nancy serves a plateful of homemade peppernut cookies. "What's been amazing," says Nancy, "is the park staff tell me there is never any vandalism on these trees." She planted a Red Oak to remember Krista in a nearby neighborhood park where she once played with Susan and Jefferson. We love knowing this dramatic tree will provide families shade in our hot summers for years to come!

Like MacKerrow, most parents seek to connect the legacy with some natural expression of their child. For Babs Egolf, whose son was a hands-on learner, she and her husband find immense pleasure in providing a community college scholarship for graduates entering vocational trades. "Our son didn't have academic interests, but loved welding. So we look for young people with passion. It's even OK to have poor grades," says Babs. "So far we've supported Priest River high school students in diesel mechanics, welding, millwright and carpentry. My favorite part is the interviews when we meet other young people like Wade."

"When someone suggested planting a cherry tree at the local church in memory of our seven-year-old son JD (Joshua Dean), his ten-year-old cousin Jordon overheard and protested," recalls JD's mother, Cheryl Hillis. "I think JD would think a tree sucked," said Jordon, to the surprise of his family. When the family asked Jordon what he had in mind instead, he said, "The basketball court at the Boys and Girls Club where he hoped to play someday sucks [a favorite word of Jordon's]. We should build a new one and name it after him." Jordon and his older brothers spent all their spare time in this run-down, inner-city gym and knew the hazards of the old chipped linoleum tile court. When the family suggested how expensive an endeavor this might be, Jordon responded by simply saying, "Well, all I am saying is that if you want to do something for JD, he would want a court." The drive for JD's court was born.

"What he loved was basketball . . . day in and day out," recalls Dave Hillis, his uncle. A healthy, outgoing, sports-oriented boy, he was engaged in a fast game of basketball at his uncle's house when he suddenly collapsed. They rushed him to the hospital. Within hours, the stunned family learned he suffered an Arteriovenous Malformation (AVM), which led to a massive brain hemorrhage. They spent the night praying and crying, holding out hope for a miracle. The next morning doctors gently insisted that there was no hope. The family took him off life support and watched the child they all considered "a pixie from heaven" die.

JD grew up in a family of males. His father was one of three brothers, and their families gave birth to eight sons and one daughter. They chose to live near each other in the inner city of Tacoma, Washington. The neighborhood was rife with gang activity, drug use, and single parents struggling to raise children safely. They believed that a "ministry of presence" could be part of their positive contributions to the community. In their years of living in Hilltop the three families made many friends. "What the Hilltop area didn't have were enough healthy sports options for kids," recalls his Uncle Dave. "Inspired by Jordon, we decided to invite the community to help us restore the Al Davies Boys and Girls Club basketball court/gym." The brothers spent four months fundraising, gaining support from radio and newspaper coverage, foundations and individuals, with donations ranging from twenty-five cents from children, to $20,000 grants. They dedicated the $110,000 brand-new maple wood court, six new baskets, and score boards as the JD Hillis Memorial Court.

"It gave the men in the family a concrete project to work on that they knew would bring pleasure to so many other children and honor JD," recalls Cheryl. Each Christmas the gym hosts a JD Hillis Memorial basketball tournament for young children aged eight to fifteen, a major community event. "It is sheer pleasure to drop by during some of the games and see all this youthful energy directed in positive ways . . . clearly healing for all of our family," said Cheryl.

After visiting Mongolia, the Girvins decided to establish a scholarship program for children of low-income nomad families to receive a university education. Friends and family helped build the fund, and George and Lila find deep satisfaction knowing there are now graduates in social work, education, and the medical field giving service to the country Matthew loved.

It's not uncommon for these endeavors to grow and draw others into the cause. In fact, a common denominator among many nonprofit organizations is that the founders are not persons with exceptional financial means. But they carry a passion born of love that proves inviting to others. When they articulate a clear and viable vision, this gives others who loved the child a positive way to come alongside a family.

Gretchen Holt Witt turned her grief into public awareness and research funding, one cookie at a time. This New Jersey mother's idea to bake cookies began after her three-year-old son Liam finished his cancer treatments. "I wanted to come up with something that was so easy anybody could do it anywhere—something so innocent and warm and friendly and inviting that people couldn't turn away." In the early years, Gretchen and her volunteers baked 96,000 cookies and raised $420,000 for pediatric cancer research. "The awful twist is that we started this when Liam was cancer free, and then we lost him. So as much as I would like to curl up in a ball and cry, I have to do it for him." She finds this effort empowering. Today, this grassroots organization (cookiesforkidscancer.org) helps people set up bake sales across the country, sending 100 percent of profits to fund the fight against pediatric cancer.[1]

Always after national tragedies, we see communities unite in creative efforts to offer positive energy amid sorrow. Within weeks after the national tragedy in Newtown, Connecticut, where a lone gunman killed twenty children and six adults at Sandy Hook Elementary School, parents and others in this community channeled their grief into the formation of grassroots organizations. Besides holding individual family memorials, parents united with others and founded both the Sandy Hook Promise and the Newtown Action Alliance. Concerned with both escalating gun violence, mental health issues, and school safety, they are lobbying for cultural and legislative change to build safer communities.

It has been a family ritual since our children were little that Jim and I light candles in cathedrals and churches for them whenever we travel. So when Jim arrived with Whitworth

University students in San Salvador after Krista died, he visited the newly restored cathedral in hopes of saying special prayers. To his dismay, the church removed the candles during the remodel. The following morning he took students to La Divina Providencia. This historic site commemorates the former Archbishop of San Salvador, Oscar Romera. On March 24, 1980, just as Romero lifted his arms to lead a blessing of communion bread and wine, assassins killed him. It's widely believed that his support for the poor, interest in liberation theology, and open radio appeals to soldiers to stop fulfilling government repression of human rights led to his killing from alleged government death squads.

Jim always found this visit to introduce students to Archbishop Romero's story meaningful. In this small chapel, he found candles available to light for Susan and Peter, Jefferson, and Aaron. Then he lit a candle for Krista and found himself flooded with earlier memories of being here with her. He left the group, sat outside on the grass, and had the deepest cry he'd had in a long time. "I broke down and wept and felt a release of emotions I'd bottled for months. It's like all that I had held in reserve finally poured out," he recalls.

Shortly before Jim left for Central America, we received a beautiful handmade card from author Isabel Allende. I'd sent her an essay I'd written about Krista after reading her poignant memoir *Paula*, written about the agonizing illness and death of her beautiful, married daughter, also in her twenties. In Allende's note, she wrote that she had cried with us as she read Krista's similar story of a young husband left, a beautiful life lost. "I hope you'll have sweet dreams about Krista," she wrote. This is something we rarely had. The evening after his La Divina Providencia experience, Jim had his first sweet dream of Krista, a vivid image of her as a child coming to him.

His experience in El Salvador has profoundly shaped our lives. He called me the next morning and said, "We've got to do something in memory of Krista besides cry." I'd actually been thinking along similar lines while tearing up the lawn, amending the soil, and planting a new garden. "When you get home, honey, let's dream together."

"We've got to do something in memory of Krista besides cry."
—*Jim Hunt*

So, after Jim returned home from Central America, we began brainstorming what we might create to honor Krista's dreams and memory. We first considered what had been her strong interests and actions before her life ended. In her written application to MCC, she expressed that her choice for volunteer service was motivated by her desire "to show God's love in actions." The journals Krista kept as an inner-city biology teacher in Tacoma, Washington, and while in Bañado illustrated how central she found prayer. It provided a vibrant grounding for daily strength in hard places.

But she also felt unsure about her future, pondering which graduate programs and career directions fit her best. Like many young adults in their twenties, she debated different professional possibilities. Krista and Aaron's director at MCC in Bolivia was an attorney. Conversations with this mentor likely influenced one of her last journal entries where she mentions contemplating law school.

> 4-18-98: I had an epiphany the other day. I thought how cool it would be to be a free-lance peace/justice lawyer working on things ranging from alternative youth punishment/sentences to working on labor disputes and home costs. Or work for law firm that allows ½ time on poverty/justice issues. Ideas: immigrants/labor/children/youth.

Clearly she hoped this season of volunteering in Bolivia might bring clarity to her confusion. In preparation for graduate school, she withdrew $500 from their savings earned in Alaska to take a long-distance course from the University of Washington.

Then we evaluated our own skills and limitations. We recognized how much support students receive throughout elementary, high school, or college. When they enter their twenties, "they hit the abyss," said Sharon Parks, whose book *Big Questions, Worthy Dreams* addresses the unmet needs of young adults. In contemporary America, they seldom follow historic traditions of early marriage, career, and family. "Young adults often lack significant mentoring support during the pivotal twenties when they make important choices about faith, values, relationships, and career paths," Parks observed.

We also knew that some young adults, similar to Krista and Aaron, choose to give a year or more to voluntary service. In 1999, long-term volunteerism was often not widely valued by parents or our culture. "You want to work for free?" lamented more than one parent who had sacrificed for years, often carrying second jobs to pay for the high costs of college. Voluntary service, especially in places where suffering and injustice prevail, inevitably raises unsettling questions around justice, economics, theology, and meaning. After years of exploring the upheaval in world views with students returning from Central America, Jim believed young adult volunteers also needed communities where they found support for the questions that service engenders.

If we could offer a mentoring community to encourage young adult leaders who chose a sustained time of service, it would offer a natural legacy of Krista's hopes. Because we lacked significant start-up funds, we wrote to all the friends and family who had sent comforting condolence cards. We shared our vision and asked for help. This gave everyone who loved Krista and felt so deeply saddened by her death a positive place to put their energy.

From their generous responses emerged the founding of the Krista Foundation for Global Citizenship, a 501c3 educational foundation. The foundation encourages and supports young adults doing service in America's inner cities, in developing nations, and with environmental projects, all areas of Krista's interests. Working with existing agencies, such as the Peace Corps, Jesuit Volunteers, AmeriCorps, or Lutheran Volunteer Corp, all Krista Colleagues serve in "hands-on" action.

We began with nine young adults in the charter class of 1999. "Many of us knew Krista, so we weren't naive to the dangers of service, and really valued the extra support," recalls Valerie Norwood, who volunteered with her husband, Tom, outside of Nairobi, Kenya. Aaron, also in the Charter class, chose to return to Bolivia to fulfill their original dream of three years of service. However, rather than return alone to their remote village, he moved to Santa Cruz. Here he began an innovative micro-finance program for poor women. Each year fifteen to eighteen new Krista Colleagues join the community, and we cherish the friendships with such other inspiring young adults. Remembering Krista's need for $500 to further her skills, we also included a $1,000 service-leadership grant to develop their talents. Starting the Krista Foundation also became the source of my gradual reentry into the life of the wider community. As I became executive director, I found myself so energized in this creative effort that solitude no longer seemed essential.

But starting a nonprofit legacy is only one way of creative remembrance. Nor is it a feasible or desirable choice for many families. Staying open to our creative sides during sorrow often opens our hearts to enter other unexpected experiences. Expressing oneself through journal writing, painting, music, sports, woodworking, scrapbooking—or absolutely any enjoyable activity that absorbs our interest—can ease our journey. When Sheree Capulli avoided leaving home after her son's death, she did stay in contact with a close friend since grade school. Dawn, an artist, suggested they make a T-shirt quilt with his favorite shirts, something hands-on. Dawn taught Sheree how to quilt, and they set a goal to have it accomplished by the first year anniversary of her son's death. Sheree found the tangible touch of fabric, the faithfulness of her friend, and the delight in learning a contemplative skill calmed her spirit.

Staying open to our creative sides
during sorrow often opens our hearts to
enter other unexpected experiences.

For seven months, Lila Girvin painted to prepare for a show. Afterward, she found less desire to paint and turned to playing the piano again. "A friend played a keyboard and offered to come over regularly and play alongside me. It turned into a marvelous discipline, something I had to do."

One need not be a professional artist or musician to discover the healing benefits of creativity. "Creativity is a manifestation of gratitude for our lives and the world around us," believes Ann Walker, art therapist in an innovative program at Spokane's Sacred Heart Medical Center and Children's hospital. "At the same time, it also allows for the expression of emotions we would often rather avoid like guilt, shame, sadness, and anger. When we can get those emotions out on paper, they no longer eat at us from the inside, and we can let them go. That's the power of the creative process."

Walker also believes it doesn't matter what something looks like in the end. "It's what happens in the process of creating, the expression of emotion, the personal insights attained. That's how creativity is life-changing." As the "art lady" at the medical center, she rolls in an "art cart" to children in life-threatening illnesses and witnessed many instances where gloom and pain become joy and fun through creativity. She believes firmly in the power of art to heal. "The artistic process reaches nonverbal areas of the brain and allows us to express and work through aspects of our lives that hinder us. It definitely increases our sense of well-being."[2]

A couple of years after starting the Krista Foundation, another creative effort absorbed our attention. A dilapidated barn once housed eighteen chickens, two pygmy goats, Dutch bunnies, even Krista's Palomino horse while the children were growing up. As the Krista Foundation grew, we needed places to gather for conferences, board meetings, and debriefing retreats. We began to imagine a guest house to replace the red barn, a "place" that cements an "idea." We knew that young adults in their twenties often feel uprooted, especially those engaged in service around the world. Sometimes their families also enter transitions as they become "empty nesters," moving homes, or even settling in new cities. We sensed a guest house where Krista Colleagues and the Board of Directors could gather would greatly enrich this mentoring community.

After tearing down the old barn, we decided to have a "blessing of the builders and artisans." With the warm glow of tiki torches around the perimeter, we invited friends to join us. That evening a friend told us of someone who placed prayers in the foundation of their new home. "You might want to do this too," he suggested. So we sent an e-mail to Krista Colleagues and prayers came in from around the world. We printed these off, folded them up, and placed them all around the floor of the rooms. The next morning the burly cement pourers arrived.

"What are these?" they asked. We explained that Mother Teresa, Bishop Tutu, and many personal prayers were included in hopes this might become a sacred, peaceful, and joyful space for others. A few weeks later, the cement pourers asked if they could drop by with their wives to show them this peaceful place. Because of our global citizenship theme, we created African, Latin American, and Northwest bedrooms, plus an Asian meditation area and a library. We called it the

Hearth, a word that includes heart, earth, hear, and art, plus evokes the sense of warm welcome we wanted. Others helped. Spike Grosvenor, a Whitworth faculty colleague and art professor specializing in stained glass, offered to design the Krista Foundation logo in antique European glass. When sun pours through the exquisite logo encircled in the large stone fireplace wall, a rainbow of colors dance on the floor. The Celtic prayer we once used in thank-you notes to friends after Krista's death hangs on a wall.

> Deep peace of the running wave to you
> Deep peace of the flowing air to you
> Deep peace of the quiet earth to you
> Deep peace of the shining stars to you
> Deep peace of the Son of Peace to you

At age ten, Krista spent a lot of time in the barn with her horse Amigo and a good friend, Julienne Gage. A far more confident and skilled rider than Krista, Julienne and her horse often won awards in 4-H shows. One day the two girls discovered a can of white paint. Dipping into the paint, they put their small handprints randomly around the barn, something Jim and I found charming even then. We saved the large barn door, and Kathy Peterson, an artist friend, added Krista's favorite white daisies, a maple tree, and our local quail around the girl's small handprints. We added this whimsical door to the entryway and saved many of the horse stall boards decorated with handprints for an interior craft room. Now, whenever we walk in, there's a charming reminder of Krista that makes us smile.

To build the Hearth also meant we needed a mortgage again, just as we had almost paid off our original home. But both Jim and I felt aligned on this decision. Nor did we take this harmony for granted. One of the first warnings we received after Krista died came from a father, a scientist, who lost a son. "Be aware that almost 80–90 percent of marriages fail after a child dies," he said authoritatively. Needless to say, this news upset me. The last thing I wanted to lose was a marriage I cherished. My training as a researcher kicked in later as I wondered, "Where did he get this fact? Is it verifiable?" However, it seemed feasible in light of the stress and bewilderment that couples feel. Years later I read this commonly tossed-about statistic is an urban myth. Research from Compassionate Friends placed divorce among parents who lose a child closer to a low 16 percent, a radically different outcome.[3] Researchers attribute the sustaining nature of these marriages to parents' awareness that only their spouse can fully understand the deeply shared love and loss of a child. However, they don't address the quality of the marriages that remain.

Research from Compassionate Friends
placed divorce among parents who lose
a child closer to a low 16 percent,
a radically different outcome.

Imagining how to create a space that enhances community life captured our energy. We found our days more joyful working alongside very talented people who helped us make choices around architectural design, fabrics, paint colors, function, and furnishings. A favorite moment was finally finding a hearth table, a centerpiece for imagined conversations. For months, we looked in antique stores for a long rectangle harvest table with an aged patina. We became dismayed by the dismal choices or high prices. Then, a local store brought in long plank tables created out of beautifully restored old Irish distillery floorboards. One was the perfect size for our room. We celebrated our first meal at Thanksgiving, and Jim and Grandma toasted the table with their favorite Irish Guinness beer.

Although built primarily for Krista Colleagues to use, through the years the Hearth has welcomed many other groups in the community, both friends and strangers. Still, the moments that give us the deepest satisfaction are the times with Krista Colleagues. With world music often in the background, we hear them engaged in animated conversations about the important choices in their lives, building friendships, laughing, singing, sharing their stories of service and their quest to make sense of all they've experienced. These moments make the Hearth feel like a sacred lively space.

A Celtic Rune of Hospitality is now framed in the dining area.

> I saw a stranger yestreen
>> I put food in the eating-place
>> drink in the drinking-place
>> music in the listening-place.
> And in the Sacred Name of the Triune
> He blessed myself and my house.
>> My cattle and my dear ones.
> And the lark said in her song
>> Often, often, often
> Goes Christ in the stranger's guise.
>> Often often, often
> Goes the Christ in the stranger's guise.[4]

Through the years, the Hearth has anchored the Krista Colleague community more beautifully than we could have imagined. Another creative effort lightened the sorrow. After completing my doctoral dissertation on Helga Estby and her daughter's walk across America in 1896, I planned to revise this as a book for the general public. Helga was an ordinary American woman who lived with extraordinary courage, and I believed her story deserved to be part of our historical record. As a history major at the University of Washington, I rarely read of women or minorities. We primarily studied Caucasian male military, government, or business leaders. However, after Krista's death, I completely dropped this project for three years even though publishers expressed strong interest. I just didn't care.

But all the mysterious unknowns around her life still haunted me. I've always believed our lives are shaped by the questions that we ask, an idea I first heard articulated by the author James Baldwin. I sought to figure out, *whatever gave this woman the courage and confidence to believe she could achieve such a monumental challenge? What made her so desperate to agree to almost impossible stipulations in her contract?* No unescorted women had ever achieved such a feat. Later I became fascinated with the question, *whatever caused her story to be intentionally silenced for almost 100 years?* This led to my further research interest in the silencing of family stories.

Finishing this compelling story and working with editors on suggested revisions required focus and commitment. Sorrow still marked each day, but the creativity and love required in teaching, working with the Krista Foundation and Colleagues, and writing *Bold Spirit: Helga Estby's Forgotten Walk across Victorian America* continued to ease the loss.

But by far, the most creative change in our family came in 2004 with the birth of our first grandson, Hunter Stevens, to our daughter Susan and her husband, Peter. Two years later, our son Jefferson's wife, Kris, gave birth to our first granddaughter, Erin. We acutely sensed the loss of future grandchildren from Krista and Aaron, and having a new generation of children to cherish gave us enormous hope for the future.

"I feel like we will always face each day with sorrow and love side by side," I told Jim one night, a few years after her death. "But I'm so thankful for all the good and happiness that still fills our days. Sometimes it amazes me." A man of quiet steady love, his eyes brimmed with tears as he held me close; there was no need to say words to show he shared a similar emotion. We knew we had survived a shipwreck together.

Chapter 10

DESIGNING RITUALS OF MEANING

*You don't need to "close" pain in order to live life
again . . . you don't need to "attain closure" to heal.*
—Nancy Berns, author of *Closure*

❧

QUESTION: IN WHAT WAYS ARE SOME FAMILIES RESHAPING THE
EMOTION-LADEN DAYS OF THE DEATH ANNIVERSARY, BIRTH-
DAYS, MOTHER AND FATHER'S DAY, CHRISTMAS, OR OTHER
HOLIDAYS INTO LIFE-AFFIRMING DAYS OF REMEMBRANCE?

"Our world came crashing down around us when our son was stillborn," remembers sociology professor, Nancy Berns, who finds "we're still picking up the pieces years later." Prior to her baby Zachariah's death in 2001, she was engaged in teaching and researching grief, bereavement, and criminal justice. But her profound personal loss became the lens for her ongoing grief-narrative research. This resulted in the compelling book *Closure: The Rush to End Grief and What It Costs Us*. She still recalls the most hurtful words after her son died. "Someday this will just be a memory," a friend tried to assure her. "That was what I most feared. I wanted my child, not a memory."[1]

As the years passed, many encouraged her to "move on" from grief. People often assumed she had already done so, an experience that sometimes left her lonely and disconnected from others. But it also caused this bright scholar to investigate and question society's contemporary emphasis on "closure" and why this popular language proves so disheartening, even destructive to many. She found no one definition of "closure" but notes that typically "closure rhetoric echoes finality. Closing a door. Bringing something to an end. Finishing a process."[2] Yet parents don't want a death to be the end of their story. Instead, they often seek new ways to continue their forever love. For many, occasional rituals of remembrance help ease their pain and contribute to learning to live in a healing space that holds both joy and sorrow.

"Closure rhetoric echoes finality. Closing a door. Bringing something to an end. Finishing a process." Yet parents don't want a death to be the end of their story.
—Nancy Berns

Berns observed that the dominant theories on grief in the twentieth century focused on "letting go," "detaching from the deceased," and "moving on." Then in the 1990s, the concept of "detaching" began to fade, but the term "closure" grew in prominence. She argues that "closure" is a made-up concept, a frame to explain how we should respond to loss. It holds the appeal of pain ending, almost in a moment in time. She illustrates how the emotional concept of closure even entered the language in national television sitcoms and criminal shows like *Friends*, *Frasier,* and *Law and Order*. After national tragedies, such as the Oklahoma bombing, Columbine, 9-11, and Katrina, it also emerged in heated political debates, especially around the nature of public memorials and arguments favoring the death penalty. "It changed from a relatively unknown term to a 'new emotional state' for explaining what we need after trauma and loss and how we should respond," said Berns.[3] However, many people in grief insist that this description has little to do with the messiness of human reality, a group she refers to as Myth Slayers. They claim, "It's not possible, not good, not desired, and not necessary," in recognition that one can't tie up grief neatly, although pain eases in time.

One concern of Berns is how difficult this makes it for persons to imagine other ways of handling profound loss. She wants people to know that there are many ways to grieve and that healing does not necessarily require closure. She believes that this "made-up" emotional state adds a false hope and pressure "to find" closure. This leads some in mourning to expect such closure will happen in weeks or months. Worse, when it doesn't, they or others around them often believe they are "stuck" in grief.

Anna Quindlen, in an essay in the *New York Times*, concurs on the limits of closure language. "The world loves closure, loves a thing that can, as they say, be gotten through. This is why it comes as a great surprise to find that loss is forever, that two decades after the event there are those occasions when something in you cries out at the continuous presence of an absence."[4]

Instead, what many grieving people discover is a desire to continue the bonds they have with a loved one, not end them. The continuing bonds theory emphasizes people do not just let go and move on, but they hang on to the bonds to the deceased by transforming the relationship. Babs Egolf understands. "When you integrate your child into your life, the loss changes significantly," said this mother who lost her only child when he was sixteen.

> At first, when Wade died, the loss felt completely outside and I was missing him terribly. But then something wonderful happened; it's like I turned around and he came back inside me. I first sensed this when I traveled to India for four months. Without the familiar sites of his bedroom at home, I felt disoriented, wondering, 'Where is he?' But then I recognized he lives inside me now and I can never lose him . . . even in the Himalayas.

"The loss is quite different now," she said, amazed at this change. "It's like we became one."

Other cultures offer customs and traditions that assume and nurture this ongoing relationship with ancestors and loved ones who have passed away. Closure? Not even considered desirable! I remember first encountering the Latino celebration of *Dia de los Muertos*—the Day of the Dead—while traveling in Central America. Indigenous people of Mexico began practicing this hundreds of years ago as they viewed death as the continuation of life rather than the end. After the Spanish arrived and began converting people to Roman Catholicism, this national holiday was moved to coincide with All Saints' Day and All Souls' Day. November 1 usually honors children and infants, the *Dia de los Inocentes* (Day of the Innocents) or the *Dia de los Angelitos* (Day of the Little Angels), while November 2 is the Day of the Dead to remember others. Families build home altars or gather at grave sites they decorate with marigold flowers, Christian crosses, the Virgin Mary, pictures, and favorite foods of the deceased. In cemeteries aglow with candles, people often stay for companionable hours sharing memories, praying, enjoying music, feasting, and partying. This tradition encourages families to take intentional time to remember. For some, they also carry the hope that the souls of their loved one will visit for a few hours, offering comfort in loss.

Other cultures offer customs and traditions that assume and nurture this ongoing relationship with ancestors and loved ones who have passed away.

I remember the first time I saw the decorated sugar skulls, dancing and humorous skeletons, toys, and pastries shaped in symbols of death in stores and bakeries. I didn't understand this vibrant, yet strange, celebration. Nor did I understand what an important avenue this offered for remembering those who have been loved. Other cultures understood and adapted this holiday, which has spread throughout Central and South America and Europe. Cities with large Latino populations in the United States now sponsor Day of the Dead festivities, often giving immigrants a way to continue this comforting ritual. Jim thought the Bolivian custom of wearing black for a year after an important death also gave a wonderful signal that you are living with loss.

The United States has set aside Memorial Day as a national holiday for families and cities to honor those killed in military service. However, for most Americans, this long weekend primarily signals the start of summer, with family gatherings, fireworks, trips to the beach, or shopping. Dwelling on the deceased rarely is encouraged in our national life.

The lack of ritual trouble some as they experience important deaths. "I recognize lately that I need a place to put my emotions, a way to tangibly act on my grief," said one woman who has lost several family members in the last three years. "I think it would offer me comfort during the grief process, and a way to show respect. But our family and, really our culture, does very little in remembrance. It seems like a void." With the birth of two grandchildren, she's becoming more conscious of the continuity of life, especially as her father's death is also imminent. "I also wonder if it wouldn't be comforting to a person facing death to know they could count on being remembered through specific rituals." Her eyes teared up as she said, "But we do nothing in our family."

The Yizkor Memorial Service celebrated by Jewish families around the world acknowledges the importance of such rituals. *Yizkor* means "remembrance," and four times a year, during High Holidays in Jewish tradition, the deceased are specifically remembered in synagogue services and in homes. Laurie Horn always finds meaning while attending these High Holiday Yizkor services as she remembers her daughter Casey who died from Familial Dysautonomia, a Jewish genetic disease, at eight-years old. "At home we also light a Yahrtzeit (sometimes called a soul candle) candle for the anniversary of Casey's death. This burns for twenty-five hours during these times of remembrance." In her forties, Laurie and her husband chose to have two more children. This pattern of remembrance has also opened up natural ways to talk to their other children about the sister they never knew. "I love that my daughter now often asks me at bedtime to tell a story about Casey. 'What was her favorite food, what colors did she like, who were her friends' . . . just natural curiosity. So Casey is still always part of the fabric of our family life."

But she doesn't feel limited to their religious ceremonies and has created her own yearly remembrance when she goes to the cemetery on Casey's birthday. "It's a beautiful place, and I sit and tell her everything about the past year. Whatever is happening with her brothers and sisters, highlights and troubles we've experienced, vacations, the work I'm doing on behalf of other children and parents suffering from this disease, just anything." She often brings a close girlfriend whose son is still living with the disease that took Casey's life. "I leave feeling very contented; it's therapeutic."

Many families create bonds that can be continued by designing occasional rituals of remembrance. By ritual, I simply mean some set of actions that are usually performed for their symbolic value. Often these are done with others, which create a space where friends and family can remember together. But other times such customs are private and help meet spiritual or emotional needs for the one in mourning. These provide a healthy way to keep their love alive, while still going forth with their lives. Such symbolic gestures also give parents, siblings, family, and friends a memorable way to honor a child. These become especially important when significant dates loom close, like a birthday or the anniversary of the child's death. Such days sometimes cause a heightened sense of grief and anxiety. "I used to dread the weeks coming up on a significant holiday, but over time I discovered my anticipation was worse than the day itself," said one mother, several years after the death of her son. She found that developing a few intentional rituals of remembrance became a kind of soothing balm.

Many families create bonds that can be continued by designing occasional rituals of remembrance.

Some find birthdays are especially hard. As the date for Cameron's twenty-first birthday loomed, Jan Skaggs invited Cameron's school friends for dinner at a favorite restaurant of hers. "We gave them each a present from Cameron's things, such as books she had underlined, favorite jewelry or scarves, music from her collection. We tried to anticipate what might be most meaningful for her friends. Rather than a time of depression, her birthday turned into a magical night of laughter, storytelling, and appreciation for how friends loved her deeply."

When Sheree Capulli neared the birthday of her son Chris after his death at age sixteen, she wrote to her large extended family and asked if they could send some memories of him. "It was summer, so we made a picnic and our immediate family went to the gravesite, and we read all the fun letters from his cousins and aunts and uncles. "I'll never say 'see you next summer' so casually again," reflected one niece, recalling her last words to Chris at their yearly reunion. "It makes me remember to treasure family." His brothers and sisters liked this opportunity of being able to talk about Chris together, so now on his birthday they usually go to his favorite Greek restaurant for dinner. "We can still tell stories of Chris, laugh together, and enjoy the family we still have."

"I told Heather before she died that whenever I saw something beautiful, I would think of her."
—*Carol Koller*

For many families, Christmas is wrapped so deeply in memorable traditions that it takes conscious reweaving to keep the joy. Diana Hartvigsen faced their family's first Christmas with great trepidation after her twenty-year-old daughter Dawnya Calbreath was brutally murdered in May 1992. A disgruntled former employee killed Dawnya and another young man during their shift working at Burger King. "I couldn't imagine just going out and buying stuff after this," she recalls. So she began a tradition for the four other children in their blended family. "Dawnya loved literature and writing and won a Washington State Poetry contest her senior year in high school with a poem about Monarch butterflies. I decided to give each of her brothers and sisters a Christmas book in her memory, something I could imagine Dawnya would want to give. I thoroughly enjoyed looking for just the right one for each sibling." Some are children's books with beautiful illustrations, like *The Polar Express* by Chris Van Allsburg, *The Mitten* by Jan Brett, *Stranger in the Woods* by Sams and Stoick, and Eugene Peterson's *The Christmas Troll*. Some introduce them to the ways others celebrate, like *The Amish Christmas,* Pearl Buck's *Christmas Day in the Morning*, or *The Christmas Tree at Rockefeller Center.* "They love the books and look forward to what I might select, so I've done this now for twenty years. I always write a short blessing for them in the book too. Now they read them aloud to their own children, and it's kept the joy in Christmas and a way to remember Dawnya."

She's also developed a habit of the mind. "Whenever thoughts of Dawnya float to the surface, I let them come." She chooses to not let her fear of sadness keep her from remembering the daughter she loves.

During holidays, some families find that it's more helpful to create new experiences instead of following earlier traditions. Since eighteen-year-old Hunter Graham was killed in a jet ski accident at the family's lake cabin on Father's Day, his mother knew it would be too painful to return on the first anniversary.

"We chose to do something entirely different and traveled across Washington State to the San Juan Islands with the entire family to kayak and camp. We'd never kayaked before, yet we knew Hunter would have loved this. Kayaking in the ocean turned out to be much more physically demanding than we expected, and we arrived at our campsite exhausted. But it was a good exhaustion. Such physical and mental effort kept us from dwelling only on this as a day of loss."

Some families like to create their own special days, not related to traditional holidays. "I told Heather before she died that whenever I saw something beautiful, I would think of her," said her mother, Carol Koller. So after Heather died at twenty-two of cancer, her parents developed a yearly ritual of taking baskets of roses from their own garden to a remote beach on the Washington coast. "We pick a day that is sunny, not gloomy, when all the factors are right. We go out early in the morning and pick a basketful of roses. Then we drive three hours to Westport where she used to go with all of her friends on a church mission trip in high school. We carry these out across the dunes where there is a gorgeous driftwood cross where we once placed some of her ashes," said Carol. Neighbors also add their rose petals, and the Kollers place all these into a carpet under the cross. "It is the offering of something beautiful and alive that we have grown and nurtured. So we bring these in remembrance of her."

Almost every parent mentions the significance of photographs and videos that help keep their child's memory alive. When others send photographs to grieving families, it's a permanent and loving gift. After Jerry Sittser lost his wife, daughter, and mother in the car accident, he consciously thought of ways to keep their family narrative alive for his three remaining children. "Photos became immensely important in creating a strong story thread in our family. I made albums for each of the children, with pictures of them with their mother and grandmother since birth. In our hallway, I also designed a living legacy that showed each of them with their mother, and then ongoing pictures of the four of us continuing to grow as a family. You could walk down the hall and see the progression of vital family life. It didn't stop with the accident." Several times a year, on the day of the accident, their birthdays, and his wedding anniversary with their mother, Lynda, he writes each child a letter. "I reflect on our journey together, the pivotal family events like family vacations, graduations, going off to college, adventures in travel, now weddings, and the birth of my first grandchild." He also likes to talk with them about how he observes the continuing legacy of their mother's influence in their lives. Lynda was a talented church soloist, and each of their adult children play instruments, sing, and enjoy music.

Until recently, little attention has been given to help parents enduring perinatal loss, which includes the many families suffer-

ing from miscarriages, stillbirth, and newborn death. Researchers writing in the October 2007 *American Journal of Maternal/
Child Nursing* lamented the social isolation such deaths often
cause and demonstrated the pivotal role for health-care professionals in offering meaningful rituals in such untimely deaths.[5]
Thoughtful changes, with the encouragement and critical feedback from bereaved parents, have been occurring in recent years.

Shelly Kuney and her daughter Lorie Sawyer experienced
this pivotal care in a Seattle hospital sensitive to infant deaths.
Lori unexpectedly entered early labor and gave birth to
premature twins when she was a little less than six months
pregnant. The baby boy and girl died within minutes. "I first
saw Lori in bed with a baby in each arm, wrapped in the pink
and blue blanket I'd brought. Memories of this are still heart-
wrenching years later," remembers Shelly. For a brief period,
the nurses took the babies to bathe and then brought them back
dressed in tiny baby clothes kept on hand for such infants.
"What I remember vividly was there was no sense of hurry
in the hospital. We could all hold the babies as long as we
needed," said this grateful grandmother. With a rocking chair
in the room, the family spent the night taking turns loving little
Molly and Joseph. Lori and her husband, Ben, have two older
sons who were five and eight and wanted to have the babies
baptized. Their friend, a female pastor, came to the hospital
to conduct this significant religious ritual. "Her presence was
such a comfort," said Shelly.

The nurses took Polaroid pictures of the babies, and when
Lori and Ben left the hospital, the nurses gave them a box
with the tiny clothes they had worn. Shelly embroidered
the two blankets with the babies' names. "This was all she
had. I couldn't do much for her, so I hoped these gave her a
comforting connection."

After Lori left the hospital, she found herself with a strong
need for solitude. "I didn't want people coming over. . . . I

just needed to be alone. It's not my way to talk a lot." But what she appreciated most was the custom of friends sending condolence cards. "I had no idea how much they would mean, but it gave me my contact with the outside world. I knew people cared. I've kept every one in a basket for years." Now she finds herself giving much more attention to the words she writes to others during loss.

They believe this bonding time with their babies have helped Joseph and Molly to always be a part of their family story, important to their older sons. Even their daughter, Annie, born after the twins' death, gets involved in remembering. "They died shortly before Halloween, so on the first-year anniversary, we took balloons and the boys wrote messages to their baby brother and sister, and we released these," said Lori. "Then, when their father took the boys to get pumpkins, they asked to add two very small ones for the babies. Now it's a tradition to have five pumpkins on the porch each year in memory. Annie, seven, continues this custom now." Lori also feels that family rituals need to be natural, not forced, and recognizes that they will change over the years. Lori later became active on the board of Soulumination, a group of professional photographers in the Seattle area. They volunteer to take life-affirming photographs of a child to give an enduring legacy for parents who lose a child to terminal illness. "They even took our little Polaroids given by the nurses and magically recreated beautiful photographs for us. I will be forever grateful since we hadn't thought to take pictures."

Sometimes a spontaneous gesture happens that eases grief. For the Bakers, seven months after Stephen's death, friends invited them to join other guests for a weekend in the San Juan Islands. "The tranquility of the island was idyllic," recalls Mary Beth. "Together we shared a family picnic of fresh bouillabaisse and blackberry cobbler around a beach fire, and relished good wine and conversation." One of the guests collected natural materials from the beach and created individual driftwood and seaweed floats with votive candles. "He gave us each one and during dinner we took turns saying who we wanted to remember and why. After dinner we set them afloat in the currents of the Strait of Juan de Fuca. It was a symbolic releasing of them as we watched the tiny candle lights bobbing in the water adrift toward Canada. Stephen had sailed in these waters, so it was especially poignant for us." What Mary Beth and Dick also appreciated was that someone else initiated this magical moment and that they weren't singled out. "Everyone has losses, and to be with people with such a reverence for family, places, and nature gave us the sense of the best of community."

But rituals need not be elaborate; even simple gestures carry connection and meaning. One father began a Christmas tradition of going to the cemetery with some battery-operated Christmas lights and putting up a tree. During the holiday season, when his grief is heightened, he stops by every night on the way home. He changes batteries while having conversations with his son. On October 19, Meredith Banka plants tulips in memory of their son Gabriel, who died at twenty weeks. Then in spring, around when he would have been born, she sees the garden ablaze with beauty. Each anniversary the Bakers contribute a riot of colorful roses to their church sanctuary in memory of the three hundred roses friends brought to Stephen's memorial. "As a young man, he always gave a rose to me, his sister, and girlfriends. He could only afford one, so he found the most beautiful long-stemmed rose he could, and this tradition honors his kindness," said Mary Beth. An accomplished cook, she often bakes his favorite lemon meringue pie on his birthday.

But rituals need not be elaborate; even simple gestures carry connection and meaning.

Friends can offer small ways for a person to be remembered. Stephanie comes from a large extended farm family and her custom for this busy beauty salon owner is hosting a yearly Easter brunch. The Easter after her cousin, the father of two young children, died in an accident, she continued this tradition. They joined hands in their customary circle for a prayer before feasting and the Easter egg hunt. In her prayer, she mentioned the loss of her beloved cousin and many in the family teared up. "Afterwards, I saw his wife crying in the next room, and I felt terrible that I had upset her," recalls Stephanie. "But when I came and apologized, she said, 'Oh, no, I'm not crying because you mentioned him, but in happiness because I was so afraid you wouldn't.'"

After Sarah Bain gave birth to her stillborn daughter Grace, a friend gave them a beautiful log planter for their porch. "Each spring the other children help me plant it in memory of the baby sister they never knew. It blooms all summer in remembrance." Even years later, Arlin Migliazzo, a colleague of Jim's from the History department, sends a card of condolence each May, simply saying "We remember." Because of this, Jim felt free to talk with him over coffee about how he was honestly feeling. Such ongoing acknowledgments by friends and family offer a gesture of grace to persons in deep grief.

Our family has found that these healing gestures have given a measure of peace. Some are one-time remembrances; others are part of the continual fabric of our daily lives. Aaron, Krista's husband, decided to try the spiritual practice of fasting as a way to mark the end of his first year of mourning. Living again in Bolivia, but now in the city of Santa Cruz with a group of other volunteers, he found a "mourning partner" who agreed to join him in six days of fasting. They began the fast on the day of the accident—May 20—and continued until the day of his wedding anniversary—May 26. "Then we drove several hours to the accident site and broke the fast with communion bread and wine. Life had seemed so drab and colorless since Krista's death, so I had enrolled in flamenco classes, and we actually had our dance program the night of our anniversary. I danced with her picture close to my heart, trying to regain some of the zest and flavor of loving life again."

A festive spring ritual we began at the Hearth is an annual day of prayer for the Krista Foundation. On the May 20 anniversary morning of Krista's death, we welcome drop-in guests with home-baked orange/cranberry scones and South American coffee and tea. A small group of friends and KF supporters come by to pray for Krista Colleagues and our upcoming mentoring conference. Except for our closest friends, most guests aren't aware it's also the anniversary. Instead, we want to keep the focus on the present, especially the basket of written prayer requests sent from Krista Colleagues serving around the world. Guests select an e-mail from a Colleague and then find an Adirondack chair, library couch, or lawn swing to begin their morning with private prayers.

The long, frigid Spokane winter has ended. Instead of treacherous ice along the garden pathways, we are now greeted by the scent of white lilacs, pink daphne, and hyacinths. Hundreds of buttercup daffodils, a confetti of tulips, and star magnolias enliven the landscape. Emerging leaves of rhubarb and grapes, blossoming fruit trees, and raspberry canes give hints of summer's promise of bounty. Because we are up early baking scones and preparing the Hearth, we no longer wake at 6 a.m. feeling the shock that altered our family life forever. We're grateful the Lieberts and Frases still always come to our door on May 20. Their faithful presence adds warmth to this ritual of remembrance as we seek to live with a spirit of hope.

In recent years, Jim became intrigued with research on the impact of gratitude on daily life. "It's fascinating to read about this field of positive psychology," said Jim one night over the dinner table. Research shows that if you incorporate gratitude into your life you are more physically fit, have more friends and a more positive relationship with your spouse, and even sleep better. It makes sense." Curious, he began to keep a gratitude journal. The part I enjoy most is bedtime when he sometimes shares specific things he's grateful for during the day. It certainly made sense why a spouse would be happy hearing, "I loved walking in the door to the aroma of lasagna," or "Let me tell you about a great conversation I had with a student today." It's only an intermittent conversation, but one that's always fun when it happens.

Because rituals often involve sharing remembrances with others, these offer significant moments to release our privately held grief with companions along the journey. And though we are broken hearted, these times of honoring one we love give glimpses of light. A musician friend, Kirk Kassner, introduced me to poet/songwriter Leonard Cohen when he shared a phrase from one of his songs. I keep this by my desk, always a reminder to stay engaged in our luminous, yet troubled, world.

> Ring the bells that
> still can ring
> Forget your perfect offering
> There is a CRACK in everything
> That's how the LIGHT gets in.[6]

Creative gestures and rituals offer us a chance to ring the bells that still can ring. It's a pathway that holds the possibility of opening our cracked heart to healing light. A gentle gift to ourselves for the journey.

Chapter 11

NURTURING HOPE IN NATURE

*Everybody needs beauty as well as bread,
places to play in and pray in, where nature may
heal and give strength to body and soul.*

—John Muir, *Yosemite naturalist*

cx/xo

QUESTION: WILL TIMES IN NATURE OFFER THOSE WHO GRIEVE
MOMENTS OF RESTORATION AND HEALING?

Throughout our journey since Krista's death, both the fleeting gifts of nature and the permanent, rock-deep landscapes of the earth have offered a kind of sacramental healing and promise. These times affirm environmentalist Rachel Carson's belief that "Those who dwell among the beauties and mysteries of the earth are not alone or weary of life."[1] Plus the winsome connections to the creatures of the land continually give moments of companionship. Parents often shared stories of the power of gardens, local or national parks, and other natural spaces for healing.

"Those who dwell among the
beauties and mysteries of the earth
are not alone or weary of life."
—*Rachel Carson*

America's national forest wilderness drew Babs Egolf after her son, Wade, rolled a truck near their ranch in Idaho. In the first year she found herself almost immobilized with grief and anger and regrets. Throughout Wade's childhood, when they lived near the national forests, he had been her companion in their isolated community. He loved the mountains, hiking, hunting, and fishing. "He was a great outdoors kid," said Babs. With her only child now dead, she also felt like she lost her identity as a mother. "It felt like a demarcation in my life, almost a midlife separation from myself. I was in a liminal land of in-betweenness for a while. I felt groundless with nothing solid to stand on. I was totally incapacitated and I functioned on automatic pilot."

But the next summer, she and her husband embarked on a garden project that provided a focus for their grief. "This gave us a purpose to celebrate Wade and also do physical work. Being out in nature and the forest with my husband allowed us to communicate and open up." They decided to gather rocks from all the forest roads that Wade loved and build a path on their ranch land. Every weekend, they drove their pickup into the Kaniksu National Forest looking for just the right rocks of indigenous granite and shale.

At first, Babs found this problematic because she wanted her husband to grieve in similar ways to her. "We actually approached the project very differently. My husband had a goal and wanted to go to the top of the mountain and then drive down. I wanted to stop all along the way, whenever we found a rock worth considering. I thought the process was what mattered. This was a journey."

They worked this out and in a few weeks built a beautiful pathway. They found a tile artist who made a landing tile with all of Wade's favorite items: South Baldy Mountain, a shotgun, flushed grouse, wetlands, a helmet, four-wheeler, and tiny trillium. They placed a small Buddha nearby and engraved Wade's name on a stone.

Creating the garden became just the first proactive step in Bab's journey through grief. She eventually chose to finish her college degree, attended silent retreats, and even studied in India for a four-month period. "When Wade died, my faith came into question. There was no explanation for his death, and I lost all faith in a divine presence in life. I had to live with groundlessness. Nothing seemed solid. His death was like a rug pulled out, especially as a mother of an only child, since I was no longer a mother. Sand, not rock, was under my feet."

To explore her spiritual questions, she traveled to Sikkim, the traditional original Buddhist capital in the independent Buddhist kingdom. "This allowed me to discover a spiritual core in a powerful way. The people there just lived and breathed a sense of the sacred. They'd start their morning rituals to mountains, rocks, trees, mountains, water. There's such an intersection of spirituality, mythology, and life in the culture."

For Carol Koller, whose daughter Heather struggled through cancer, the fourth bout proved especially painful. Shortly after she graduated from Pacific Lutheran University, the ravaging rhabdomyosarcoma kept mutating and returned with a vengeance. Within months it became clear that Heather was dying. So her mom and dad brought her to their newly built home in Vancouver, Washington, where they recently moved. They needed to be near Carol's position as a fundraiser for medical research.

They created a home for Heather in their great room. With grand windows looking out onto a barren dirt lot, they all imagined how it could be transformed into a bountiful garden. Heather wanted to help plan it and spent hours poring over garden design magazines. With over a half acre of land to fill, Heather listed specific species of the twenty-eight trees, vibrant Dutch tulips, and dozens of rose bushes she wanted planted in spring.

After her daughter's death, Carol found, "The garden saved my life. I could pour myself into something that was ongoing, living, and responded to nurture." During the next five years, she and her husband, Brant, climbed into their pick-up and spent weekend hours at nurseries from Seattle to Eugene. "We were on a hunt for the forty-eight roses, thirty-five specimen peonies, and other plants that Heather liked." Back home, they dug holes, created hillside pathways, and eventually planted twenty-eight trees in the garden they named "Heatherwood."

"Her spirit and planning was in it. Our time in the garden created something beautiful as a reflection of our love for her. I remember Heather often in the silent things . . . the wonderful happenings in the garden, the edge of the sunset, an early morning sunrise, the opening of a Peace rose, the small buds on the heather, seeing the light and shadows play. For years, we just would go outside and look and feel and be."

Then one day they needed to move out. "I never looked

back," said Carol. "We left it as a gift for the next owner because I couldn't pull it apart."

One of the hallmarks of grief is our yearning for some kind of reconnection with a child. "Searching, or yearning, crops up in nearly all the contemporary investigations of grief," says Meghan O'Rourke. Recent research found that "the feeling that predominated in the bereaved subjects was not depression or disbelief or anger, but yearning," she writes in a *New Yorker* article. "Nor does a belief in heavenly reunion protect you from grief."[2]

Many a parent spoke of an experience in nature that provided a comforting sense of connection. Most don't try to explain it rationally; it just happened. What seems consistent is the inner solace that such mysterious moments give, often enhancing their sense of peace.

"Searching, or yearning, crops up in nearly all the contemporary investigations of grief. . . . The feeling that predominated in the bereaved subjects was not depression or disbelief or anger, but yearning. Nor does a belief in heavenly reunion protect you from grief. "
—*Meghan O'Rourke*

When a child is a young adult and moves away from home, they grow in ways parents often don't see or experience. Jan Skaggs' daughter Cameron was killed one evening at a crosswalk near her Spokane, Washington, campus in her sophomore year. Discovering new facets of Cameron's life compounded both joy and sorrow. The one steady thing Jan did afterward was to pause and journal a lot. This discipline gave her short moments of reflection and remembrance and anchored her days. After pouring a cup of tea, she'd go to Cameron's bedroom to sit in a rocking chair. Cameron's childhood had been difficult, with the divorce of her parents when she was one year old. She also struggled with Noonan's syndrome, a hereditary condition that results in an unusual physiognomy, with small stature, broad shoulders, and almost no hips. "She was socially behind her peers, yet with an exceptionally bright intellect. High school was painful, with years of rejection. She also had a conflicted relationship with her biological dad." Jan savored the poetry Cameron wrote and saw a courageous side she never knew.

What became especially poignant for Jan was seeing how her daughter blossomed in college. "It felt like a climbing rose . . . they're slow the first year, creep the next, almost dormant, then they leap up a trellis and explode with hundreds of buds starting to open. I felt robbed of Cameron because she was just blossoming in beautiful ways to become the woman she could be. Just as she burst into bloom, she went over the wall to the other side."

The March afternoon of Cameron's memorial service, the Skaggs experienced a marvelous moment that still gives them wonder. As the family walked out on the porch of their Texas ranch house, they saw hundreds of yellow butterflies swirling around their garden, all inside the fence. "They seemed to be dancing around Cameron's brother's head as he watched in awe." Having lived in their hill country home for over twenty years, never before or since have they seen such abundant butterflies in March. However, on the first-year anniversary, when Jan and her husband, Harold, took a walk on their lane, a solitary yellow butterfly followed them. "It felt like an assurance from Cameron that she's OK, just as the enchantment of yellow butterflies we savored on the March day of Cameron's memorial."

When Katie McClary, a twenty-five-year-old biology graduate from Duke University died, her mother Patty planted a Canadian cherry tree in their backyard. Then she added an angel and built a blue slate and river rock garden. "She was a red-haired, passionate musician, and the tree had red leaves just like her flaming hair. We can see the tree and angel from nearly all of our rooms. I pour my morning cup of coffee and find peace just seeing this reminder of her," said her mother. She also enjoys tending Katie's cemetery plot, which is just two blocks from their home, whether washing off bird poop from Katie's headstone or picking up twigs. She values doing something tangible to care for her daughter's memory. But one of the most delightful events happened during a night when Patty found she couldn't sleep, a common problem for bereaved parents. "I was having breathing problems and awoke at 2 a.m. to a gorgeous swirling sky. It was utterly awe inspiring. Just as I was watching, I saw a shooting star . . . it felt like a sign of Katie. 'Hi, Katie,' I said, and then I was able to rest." It's this peace that such moments bring that encourages parents most.

Often, there isn't a space for gardening, or this isn't how families want to spend their limited time for relaxation or renewal. But they, too, speak of the restoration given from public spaces in nature. Whether hiking a high mountain trail, relaxing to the crash of ocean waves, going to a city beach or park, or discovering the silence and rhythm of cross-country skiing or cycling, they sense a calming renewal after being outdoors.

This proved true for our son Jefferson who returned to Prince William Sound in Alaska after Krista's memorials. Working long hours in the fishing industry with no close family or friends nearby, we asked him later how he lived with his own sadness. "After work, I'd go down and sit by the ocean . . . somehow it calmed me."

Kathleen Dean Moore, a naturalist from Oregon, encountered a season where several devastating deaths left her immersed in sorrow. So she also turned to the comfort of the wild. She wanted to learn what the natural world could teach her about sorrow and gladness. Later, she wrote a series of meditations in *Wild Comfort,* illustrating the reassurance to her soul from being in wet, wild places.

> I have felt their peace, the steady surge and flow of the sea on sand, water slipping over stones. There is meaning in the natural rhythms of dying and living, winter and spring, bones and leaves. Even in times of bewilderment or despair, there is steadfast ground underfoot—pine duff, baked clay, stone turned red in the rain. I am trying to understand this, the power of water, air, earth, and time to bring gladness gradually from grief and to restore meaning to lives that seem empty or unmoored.[3]

Such places provide a chance to pause and be attentive to ongoing life.

"I am trying to understand this, the power of water, air, earth, and time to bring gladness gradually from grief and to restore meaning to lives that seem empty or unmoored."
—*Kathleen Dean Moore*

I remember a moment in nature that stilled one of my own questions. A common dilemma parents mention is the awkwardness of meeting new people, who often ask, "How many children do you have?" However, my concern wasn't what others wanted to know. Instead, I wanted to know. *What will happen to our family dynamic now? Are we a family with three children or a family of two children now? What does this mean? Or will we always be a family of five?* One sunny afternoon, while sitting on a small beach at Priest Lake, five black and white butterflies of varying size flew near our beach chairs. They literally danced around Jim and me for ten to fifteen minutes. It's a sight I've never seen before or since, and it was answer enough for the moment.

We live on a winding lane where undeveloped land juts up a hillside behind the houses to the fertile Five Mile Prairie. Because this natural corridor goes for acres until it nears the Little Spokane River, the land abounds with wildlife. We see white-tailed deer, raccoons, squirrels, coveys of quail, pheasants (one we've named Winthrop), turkeys, and an occasional owl or blue heron. Sometimes we hear the song of coyotes howling at night. On one terrible evening they stole down the hillside to our barn and killed the two pygmy goats that seven-year-old Krista had been tenderly raising.

We bought this home primarily because it was near the college where we taught, plus the giant ponderosa pine and spruce trees that graced the land immediately enchanted us. There was no way in one's lifetime that we could grow such stately trees. After freezing winters and a late spring, we rejoice when the first tiger swallow-tailed butterflies arrive to dart amid the tulips and daffodils. Their brilliant yellow and black wings always herald the delightful days of summer.

I didn't know at first how much our garden would emerge as a central place of renewal for our family and friends. I originally discovered the healing power of working with the land during harsh treatments and recovery from breast cancer in my mid fifties. Behind our home, earlier owners built a three-tier rockery that we basically ignored while raising three children. Shortly after completing chemotherapy, I started studying about perennials and decided to develop the rock garden. I think the idea of plants that live "forever" appealed to me during this vulnerable time of fragile health. A mixed rockery of sun and shade terrain, centered with a large sixty-year-old lavender lilac, introduced me to the wonders of hostas, Autumn Joy sedum, candytuft, daylilies, and coreopsis.

In the early months of acute grief I found enormous calm and pleasure in the garden. In spring, seeing the first sliver of crocuses pushing through patches of snow, watching the slow unfurling of a star magnolia or Japanese iris, or catching the scent of white lilacs gave such promise. I loved Spokane's summers, seeing morning dew captured in the leaves of lady's mantle, a bumblebee gathering nectar on a giant allium, or tasting a sun-warmed heritage tomato off the vine. In fall, harvesting and cooking Japanese eggplants, Kentucky green beans, pungent basil, or fingerling potatoes filled our home with soothing aromas. These scents comforted. While walking amid such exquisite beauty, something good and gentle stirred inside, warming my vulnerable heart, and kept me mindful of the miracle of all living creation.

"I can garden" was the last sentence put in my journal entry on "what I can and cannot do." When Spokane's long winter snows finally thaw, the land comes alive with sunny yellow, coral, and pale butter-white bulbs. We tried dwarf fruit trees again after several earlier failures from our hard frosts and found an Asian pear that produced abundant fruit. Names of plants became important, like the "Morning Has Broken" rose, the hymn for Krista's baptism and memorial service. Jim enhanced a large compost pile. This "black gold" amends the soil and helps struggling plants thrive again. They practically smile!

For us, the garden offered a combination of interweaving gifts. I once heard that there should be a $5 investment in soil for every $1 in the plants, usually the opposite of our initial instincts as gardeners. I liked how compost could bring life to depleted soil. Knowing we lived in a deep winter of the soul, with no idea how long this interior season would last, it helped seeing the value of dormancy, waiting, and trusting that what is happening underground during the winter months is important.

I also like the randomness, where seeds scattered by birds and wind bring up serendipitous sprouts in unexpected places. Shattered by the randomness of life, yet constantly having memories of our daughter's sweet, budding, vibrant spirit, these tangible signs in the universe of life's continuity gently blessed us.

Working with soil and plants served
as a reminder that gardens flourish most
as we participate in the creation.

To augment the global citizen theme developed inside the Hearth, we attempted to create similar global gardens, if you use the term loosely! We completed the Asian garden in October, just days before our Korean son Jefferson's wedding rehearsal dinner. Their photographs taken near a brilliant fall ornamental maple tree happened just in time. Two days later frost and storms stripped all the gorgeous fall leaves. We found Mexican pottery, a chimera fireplace, and colorful plants for a Latin American patio, and we added six semi-dwarf fruit trees to the American orchard. A friend of Krista's from high school utilized the old barn wood and built a delightful red barn children's playhouse. Our attempts at an African garden never got past a few grasses and stones, along with a giraffe hand made in Nicaragua! Maybe someday we'll figure out how a cold-winter Northwest site can evoke an African motif.

Working with soil and plants served as a reminder that gardens flourish most as we participate in the creation. To continue participating in the fullness of life meant we needed to stay involved. When a garden suffers neglect, in just weeks the weeds will choke out emerging beauty. There's a quote that says "If all else fails, there's always the garden." Jim teased me about the dangers of becoming a "meliorist." His understanding of this historical term meant one removes oneself from the world and just tends his or her garden, a type of escapism. But the term actually has a different nuance. Instead, it means people believe the world will get better and humans can aid in its improvement. The improvement of society depends on human effort.

Rather than escapism, I found the opposite truth emerged after being humbled by such daily sheer wonder. If I spent time in the garden, then I could face the world with more centered peace and a lightness of being. To see a Sunset Maple blaze in autumn splendor or taste the sweet-tart spice of a blueberry or sun-ripened peach gave me a trust in the universe.

Around the same time I was creating gardens, Jim immersed himself in research and writing about naturalist John Muir. Jim has a long interest in the impact of youthful travel on emerging leadership, partly from observing how Whitworth's Central America Study/Service trip proved so life shaping for students. His research led to articles on the influence of early travel experiences in the lives of American leaders like Jane Addams, Frederick Douglass, and John Quincy Adams. After Krista's death he became fascinated with Muir's one-thousand-mile walk across the South at age twenty-nine. This preceded Muir's growing fame as an environmentalist in the Sierras, which influenced the establishment of national parks and the founding of the Sierra Club.

A botanist, Muir kept a journal during his southern journey. These included his botanical discoveries and his response to a radically different ecosystem than the Midwest of his youth. He also wrestled with theological assumptions about man's relationship to nature. In a way, Muir became a meaningful companion during Jim's years of grieving. "I became inspired by a very creative human being, his use of eloquent language, his profound insights and love of nature," said Jim. This led eventually to the publication of Jim's book *Restless Fires: Young John Muir's Thousand Mile Walk to the Gulf,* an exciting outgrowth of seven years of historical research. Growing up backpacking on the Northwest's wilderness trails, Jim resonated with Muir's belief that "all things are hitched together." He also valued Muir's commitment that all peoples have access to America's natural wild places. So for most summers, we try to visit one of our national parks.

While teaching in Whitworth's Introduction to Western Civilization course, I also found myself influenced by an environmentally sensitive writer. I loved researching and role-playing one of the remarkable twelfth-century mystics, the powerful Benedictine abbess Hildegard of Bingen from Germany. A poet, botanist, musician, and influential Catholic leader, one of her poems so expresses what nature gives.

> Glance at the sun. See the moon and stars.
> Gaze at the beauty of earth's greenings.
> Now, think.
> What delight God gives to humankind
> with all these things . . .
> All nature is at the disposal of humankind.
> We are to work with it. For
> without it we cannot survive.[4]

During these years, I also found rest in Mary Oliver's poetry and her insistence we pay attention to the marvels of each day. I reread this poem many mornings.

Why I Wake Early

> Hello, sun in my face.
> Hello, you who make the morning
> and spread it over the fields
> and into the faces of the tulips
> and the nodding morning glories,
> and into the windows of, even, the
> miserable and the crotchety—
>
> best preacher that ever was,
> dear star, that just happens
> to be where you are in the universe
> to keep us from ever-darkness,

to ease us with warm touching,
to hold us in the great hands of light—
good morning, good morning, good morning.

Watch, now, how I start the day
    in happiness, in kindness.[5]

During times of overwhelming loss, poets offer encouragement to start each day with some awareness of all that
remains. To love "that which is near at hand" includes the
generous bounty of our natural world. For without it, we can
not survive.

Chapter 12

DISCOVERING THE HEALING
POWER OF FORGIVENESS

*Forgiveness is important because it allows you to
move on. If you don't forgive, you're liable to get stuck. But
it's a process that happens over time, not instantly.*

—Babs Egolf, after she lost a sixteen-year-old
son who rolled his pick-up truck

☙

QUESTION: WHAT IS THE IMPORTANCE OF FORGIVENESS IN
EVENTUAL PEACE AND HEALING?

*O*utward rituals, those gestures that honor the one we love, usually are shared with others. An important *inward* act, which encompasses our heart, mind, and soul, is offering forgiveness. It may or may not directly involve another. Parents discuss many shades of this, whether forgiveness toward oneself, forgiveness toward another perceived as contributing to one's child's death, or forgiveness to the child whose choices caused his or her death. Or, even finding the need to release one's anger toward the Divine that such a senseless death could occur. Religious traditions, as well as medical and social science researchers, speak to the essential role of forgiveness if one desires to live without destructive bitterness and resentments.

Forgiveness is rarely easy. Nor instantaneous. Neither, in situations with violence and neglect, does forgiveness negate the demand for responsible justice. "I worry about fast forgivers," wrote Lewis Smedes, a former seminary professor, in his book *The Art of Forgiving: When You Need to Forgive and Don't Know How.* A deep believer in the essential need to practice forgiveness, nevertheless, he still cautions against instantaneous forgivers. "They tend to forgive quickly in order to avoid their pain. Or they forgive fast in order to get an advantage over the people they forgive. . . . But for serious wounds, we need to take our time."[1]

I worry about fast forgivers. They tend to forgive quickly in order to avoid their pain. . . . But for serious wounds, we need to take our time.
—*Lewis Smedes*

This makes imminent sense to Diana Hartvigsen as she has lived with knowledge of the drug-crazed man who murdered her daughter and another employee at Burger King. She sat listening to the horrific details testified to in the long trial, which led to sensationalist and extensive media coverage. "It's a long process," she said, as she looks over the past twenty years. "At first, I couldn't forgive, not even sure I wanted to. It was important to me that he owned what he did. I also wanted him to pay for the lives he took." But ten years after his conviction for the death penalty, there was another hearing to change the sentence to life in prison without parole. What happened became an important first step for Dianna. "Now, drug free, he looked us in the eye and apologized, saying he was sorry in a way that seemed genuine." Recently, she has been thinking seriously about meeting with him in prison and offering forgiveness. "I believe God calls us to forgive. I feel like this will be our final step, but I'm still a little fearful. I want my motives to be right, and hope God can use this in his life. I've been advised that God will give me the right words, and not to worry. I think I need to take this risk."

"Forgiveness gives you freedom," believes Jan Skaggs, who sought to proactively forgive a young man who accidentally killed her daughter at a crosswalk. "It's a gift to ourselves." It usually involves an intentional choice. As one person expressed, "Forgiveness is a strong move to make, like turning your shoulders sideways to walk quickly on a crowded sidewalk. It's your move."

For Aaron, an unexpected encounter in Bolivia thrust him face-to-face with the speeding bus driver and abruptly into the nexus of forgiveness. On our last day in Santa Cruz, MCC requested that Aaron meet with the lawyers and an insurance company. They needed this to allow reimbursement to MCC for Krista's death expenses and Aaron's medical injuries. He returned back around dinner time clearly distraught. "I've just spent two hours with the driver of the bus," he fumed, visibly shaking. "I even had to ride in a car with him while we went over to see another lawyer." He then described the scene.

"I didn't realize that was who he was until about halfway through," said Aaron, as he described this middle-aged man who still limped from a leg injury due to the accident. "Chris and I had been sitting next to him when we suddenly recognized that this was the bus driver. A husband and father of four children, he brought his wife along with him. I was shocked he was in the room without our being told," said Aaron. "I hadn't prepared myself emotionally for this at all."

Needing to get his bearings, Aaron quickly moved behind a desk to take a good look at the man he knew was responsible for Krista's death. "He was just three feet across from me, and I was filled with fear and uncertainty at how to respond. I found myself praying, 'Lord, help me, I don't know what I'm suppose to do or say.'" Aaron expected to feel outrage and feared he might lash out. But as he looked at the driver closely, he was surprised to feel compassion well up within himself. "Here was another human being with his own set of consequences and hurt. He looked so full of anxiety, with hunched shoulders and his head cast down. He was living with the guilt of killing three people, had lost his means of livelihood, and was obviously injured."

About an hour later, after they had finished with the lawyers, Aaron and the driver walked out to the sidewalk. "I'd been thinking of what I wanted to say to him, to express the depth of loss. I told him, 'I want you to know I hold you responsible for my wife's death. She was a good woman, and I loved her very much. She was a beautiful person.'"

Then he told the bus driver, "But because God's grace has been so generous to me, I can't do anything but forgive you." As he told us this, it was a simple statement of fact for Aaron, not feeling. He gave the one gift he could give another.

"What do I do with my anger now?" Aaron asked to no one in particular, his head buried in his hands. "I don't want to rage at God."

A faculty colleague, the parent of a teenage son, came over one afternoon and in the midst of conversation asked me, "Aren't you angry at God?" She looked like she doubted the truth to my answer when I said, "It isn't anger I feel so deeply, but sorrow." Sometimes it even surprised me that anger was not one of my primary emotions. Yet, I clearly was delighted when English department colleagues told the story of the response to Krista's death from a visiting professor from Africa. An imposing hefty 6'4" scholar, he came striding through our office hallways brimming with anger, shouting, "How can this be?" Such a random death to a young wife with her spirit of service astounded him.

Then he told the bus driver, "But because God's grace has been so generous to me, I can't do anything but forgive you."
—*Aaron Ausland*

But it was the truth. Somehow, I recognized from the beginning that if I'd known we'd lose Krista at twenty-five, I wouldn't have traded a day for the enjoyment she brought to our family life. Even during the typically difficult teenage years, we found her peer friendships, interest in jazz, debate, student government, and world issues refreshing and stimulating. A night owl, her combination of procrastination and perfectionism meant she stayed up many a late night finishing some major school report. She always wanted to begin her slow mornings with a hug. Though Jim enjoyed preparing a healthy breakfast, most often she skipped this meal while still curling her hair in front of the bathroom mirror. Sometimes she'd stop by my office at the college and we'd go out for a latte in the school hub. We laughed that this was a working mother's version of welcoming a child home after school with milk and cookies.

For us, the primary years when Krista lived within the family were already past. But for Aaron, who imagined his intimate future forever linked with the woman he'd loved since he was eighteen, her death caused significant anger. It also raised major theological questions. "About a half hour before we plunged off the cliff into the dark night air, I literally prayed, 'God, I do not fully understand prayer; it is a mystery to me. But I know you want us to come to you as children and ask. So I am asking that we do not get into an accident tonight. And if we do, that no one dies, and if someone must die, that it not be Krista,'" remembered Aaron. "I thought I knew God well enough to predict His response. I expected Him to protect us, offer us immunity and exemption from the dangers lurking in this world. When He didn't do as I asked and expected, I was confused, wounded, and angry. I was disappointed in God. When the bus rolled over the mountain ravine, most passengers were injured, but alive. Krista was one of only three who died."

Aaron knew scores of family and friends prayed for them on a regular basis. "How could God have allowed such a thing to happen when it is such a small matter for him to intervene, to answer my prayer?" he wondered. "We were the stereotypical young service-volunteer couple. We had traded in our apartment and car for a one-room mud adobe house with a bucket shower and outdoor latrine following a holy calling to live and work with the poor."

Also, with more flexible time in Bañado, Aaron had started to develop steady spiritual practices. "Each morning I sat with God for about an hour and we talked together. I thought I was getting to know God fairly well. What a surprise, then, when God held back His awesome power, retained His might, and stayed His healing hand." Left with the reality of his beloved wife's death, he concluded, "If we think that God has promised a pleasurable ride on planet Earth to those who believe, we are mistaken." Aaron wrestled honestly with these theological questions, both privately and with others, trying to sort out what he now believed. "Why in the world would I have thought it wouldn't happen? We lived in a world with many dangers," he mused as he considered his earlier grasp of the nature of God and his sense of God's favoritism.

He often stayed with us during the first year in between visits to all the significant places in their romance. With his close friend, Wakefield Gregg, he ventured back to Alaska where Krista and Aaron drove tour buses for two summers to pay off credit card and college debts before they could volunteer in Bolivia. Then he'd come back and stay awhile longer.

On one of these nights, after we had been trying for months to figure out a logo for the Krista Foundation, we sat around the dinner table. "Explain what you want to communicate," Aaron said. We mentioned that somehow we wanted the "Joy Dance" poem's sense of dynamic lightness. "We want to encourage Krista Colleagues to bring joy to the people and places where they serve." "How's this?" he asked after spending just a couple of minutes drawing on a napkin. He had turned the K and F into dancing figures within a circle. We loved it and could now take it to a graphic artist, a friend of our son-in-law Peter. He added the mountain scene behind the figures, not even knowing Krista died in a mountain ravine. Aaron worked closely with us on shaping the foundation during the early years, and we sensed it also gave him one positive place for his grief.

The book of Job took on special meaning to Aaron. Years later, he spoke at a 2003 Krista Conference about his faith journey and some of the resolutions that now gave him more peace. Since many Krista Colleagues volunteer in harsh places where suffering and injustice abound, his story has opened up their own ability to name the questions that trouble them. He became the founding editor of the Krista Foundation's *Global Citizen Journal*, published for other young adult volunteers serving around the world. By popular request, the journal published his Job address on "Musings on Suffering, Faith and Action."

By then Aaron had returned to work in Bolivia and was immersed in the deep plight of many of the poorest women and families in this impoverished nation. Seeing injustice became his daily bread. As he wrote in his introduction on "The Paradox of Suffering," he stated:

> I used to think that if you rolled up the sleeves of your mind and sweated enough synaptic juice, you could figure things out. The way I saw it, philosophical and theological ambiguity was for mental midgets, and I was determined to furrow my brow and stitch together a perfect fabric of understanding for the physical and metaphysical universe. Well, I'm no longer a sophomore and I've learned to live with unresolved tension.
>
> What killed my naive hope was the discovery that I held in my paradigm pocket two wholly inconsistent beliefs, and I was unwilling to discard either. In one hand, I clung to the belief, stubbornly, desperately, that God existed and was good and powerful and engaged with creation. In my other hand I held my own vision, newly opened to the world and freshly aware of injustice without recourse, of trampled virtue and unworthy victors. . . . I had become convinced of the suffering of innocents.
>
> What does it mean to say that God is good, powerful, aware, and engaged when the innocent suffer without just resolution? The coexistence of these ideas jarred the ordered belief system I had framed and ruined my neat thinking. This was my eternal question, the one upon which everything else hung: "How can this be?" . . . What does it mean for God and suffering to coexist and how can it be? What does the rape of a child declare about God and his hold on the universe? Pick up a paper, read the tragic headlines of war, suicide, famine, and flood and see why the world has thrown God in the dock and judged Him irrelevant.
>
> Where was God during the Holocaust? Where was God when my mother was dying of cancer and we were laying hands on her beautiful bald head and weeping over her distending body? Why was my prayer summarily ignored?

He concluded his essay with

> We should have faith because God is God and we are not. The question, "Why is there so much suffering if God is so good?" seems overwhelming, but transcending it is the question, "Why aren't God's people doing more about it when we have been so clearly called, equipped, and sent?" I don't always understand, but I know that as the Bible says, "As the heavens are higher than the earth, so are God's ways higher than my ways, and God's thoughts than my thoughts."
>
> Friends, do not let the suffering of the world challenge your faith any longer; rather, with your faith, challenge the suffering of the world. Be forgivers, reconcilers, good stewards, servant leaders, healers, peacemakers, hearers of the Word, and doers of good.

Like Aaron, I was left to reconcile my belief in God's omnipotent power to intervene and provide protection in perilous situations, and the mystery and sorrow of why God chose not to intervene for Krista. It's the quandary of praying people everywhere who lose a loved one. "I began to lose my faith in the universe," lamented one mother years after her son's death. Another mother found a different experience: "Grief taught me what faith is because faith is trusting without seeing. There was nothing to see that made sense in the death of our daughter." I found Martin Luther King Jr.'s words enlightening, reinforcing my sense that God is alongside us during such sorrow. King believes, "Our capacity to deal creatively with shattered dreams is ultimately determined by our faith in God. However dismal and catastrophic may be the present circumstances, we know we are not alone."[2]

Unlike Aaron, I didn't feel a compelling need to resolve this and probably just recognized my own limitations in understanding such a theological paradox. Instead, I tried to remember, "Was it not our Creator's love that gave us a daughter like Krista to cherish?" When I could remember this during distress, it became a doorway into thanks. When I consciously stayed thankful for her life, this seemed to ease the day and the sleepless nights. One concern we initially had was that people would give us a pat theology, like "God calls the best home" or "God wanted her in heaven." We firmly believed this was an accident, caused by human error, and trusted that God's heart broke with ours to see her death. We felt eternally grateful that no one tried to sweeten her violent death with platitudes. We also felt grateful that so many friends and family became the gentle sources of the biblical truth "Blessed are those who mourn, for they will be comforted" (Matt. 5:4 NRSV).

Sometimes the timing or the circumstances of a child's death or regrets in a parent's relationship with a child raised their own guilt and questions that called for forgiveness. "When our sixteen-year-old son died in a car accident because of his drinking, I kept asking myself, *didn't we raise him better?*" recalls Babs Egolf. They lived near the national forests, and Wade had been her companion in their isolated community. "The contentious years before his death added to our sense of loss and despair when he rolled a truck and wasn't wearing a seat belt. Questions continuously haunted me. *Did I do enough? Could I have taught him better? Was there something I didn't teach him?*" When she learned that alcohol was involved, it made her even angrier, even disconsolate. "I felt like he threw away his life."

"What I learned in pilgrimage to India is you have to bless yourself, and have acceptance that life has impermanence. . . . My challenge now is how to maintain a sense of sacredness as part of everyday life."
—Babs Egolf

At first, Babs found herself blaming herself or others. "In time, I realized that we had done most of our parenting by the time he was sixteen, and he knew our values. Nor could we blame his peer group for his going along and using alcohol. He was old enough to be responsible for his decisions. This helped release my guilt and blame," said Babs. "Over time, meditation allowed me to see my entire life, to pay attention. I took on the role of a pilgrim looking for a self-blessing, but I was looking external and outward. What I learned in pilgrimage to India is you have to bless yourself, and have acceptance that life has impermanence. Everything is always changing." She returned home from India after four months. "My challenge now is how to maintain a sense of sacredness as part of everyday life. I'm coming to realize it is found within myself wherever I am . . . when I am cooking, offering forgiveness to his friends, even with self-discipline, such as recognizing it is not appropriate to be crying in a college classroom and just dismiss myself if necessary."

For Jan Skaggs, her own earlier experiences in the importance and power of forgiveness shaped her attitude toward the young man who killed their daughter at a crosswalk. "It was a dark and rainy night," says Jan, "and Cameron was wearing dark clothes. The driver had just left the fire station where he was training in EMT, and he had a green light to turn. She had the "go" to walk, but the light was out at the crosswalk, and he never saw her."

The Skaggs flew in from their home in Texas and stayed at the Hearth for a few days. They heard how traumatized the young man was and knew he was blaming himself. "He took her death seriously, which we appreciated," said Jan, "and we heard he felt very guilty." They decided to invite him to come to the Hearth to meet. "We wanted him to know we were not holding this against him and that we forgave him. At first, his fire department mentor was hesitant to have him come because he assumed we'd want to lash out at him. He finally understood we wanted to communicate a spirit of forgiveness."

The driver was almost the same age as their daughter, Cameron. He arrived with his young wife and mother and his mentor from the fire department, and Jan and Harold greeted him at the Hearth door. They welcomed him with a hug, but he could hardly look at them. As they talked, they told him, "We know this was an accident and that you'd do anything to take it back if you could." They also encouraged him to get counseling along with his wife. "You will be forever changed, but we want you to get help and go forward in life. Otherwise your own mother will also lose a child. Please know that we forgive you."

A police investigator stood in the back of the Hearth observing the Skaggs' words of generous forgiveness. Later he said, "In all my years of working with accidents, I've never seen anything like this." Based on past experiences, Jan knew that there is freedom in forgiveness, not just to the one forgiven, but for her and their family. "We didn't want to carry bitterness along with sorrow."

Whether to oneself or others, forgiveness is a gift you give yourself. From parents' stories, most experience more of the peace they long for if they eventually make the move to forgive. When Aaron felt the surprise compassion well up in him toward the bus driver, it didn't change his sense that the speeding driver was responsible for the enormous loss of Krista in his life. But it did expand his circle of empathy beyond himself. This act opened a door toward inner peace.

CONCLUSION
Doorway into Thanks

Joy moves always to new locations,
the ease of its flow never freezing.

A long winter's tale is over. Now
with each spring day a new story.

—Rumi

❧

QUESTION: HOW CAN THE LOVE FOR ONE WE'VE LOST BECOME
A POWERFUL RESOURCE IN OUR LIVES?

On November 5, which would have been Krista's thirty-eighth birthday, we awoke to a stunning vermillion sunrise, so spectacular that Spokane citizens started sharing their awe at such radiant beauty with Facebook friends. "Linda, come see," urged my husband, Jim, who always gets up before me. "You don't want to miss this splendor."

Being attentive to such wonders often blesses and eases our days. About a year after Krista's death, I read something where a parent's comment made it sound like their grieving came to a definitive end. *Does this acute pain really ever subside?* I wondered. *Is there an actual specific day or time that grief abates?* At the time I felt like I was living in liminal space, in an in-between realm of our former life and a future I couldn't imagine. The word *limen* in Latin means "threshold," and the liminal realm describes the time and place of transition inherent in all rites of passage. After we suffer the death of one we love, we enter a threshold between our earlier life with assumptions, now torn asunder, and an unknown future. Rather than the future feeling friendly, it seems like we are in uncharted, sometimes a barren, bereft, even a hostile land. Roger Rosenblatt, a journalist, has written two poignant memoirs of the shock of losing his thiry-eight-year-old daughter, Amy, from an undiagnosed heart defect in 2007. In his latest, *Kayak Morning*, he describes grief's evolution over time. When he wrote *Making Toast* (his first book), Rosenblatt explains, "I tried to suggest that the best one can do in a situation such as ours is to get on with it. I believe that still. What I failed to calculate is the pain that increases even as one gets on with it."[1]

Does this acute pain really ever
subside? . . . Is there an actual specific
day or time that grief abates?

"No one warned me that the second year could be worse than the first, which it was for me," says Jan Skaggs, "but I wouldn't have believed it. The first year we kept having the milestones of birthday, Christmas, and anniversaries that we consciously prepared for. But the depth and breadth of our loss became vivid the second year. Cameron was the daughter from a long lineage of strong matriarchal women in Texas, now broken for good. I'll never be a mother of the bride, a grandmother to her children . . . these are irreparable losses. She also provided a glue in our family that was more powerful than we knew, until lost."

In the liminal time of deep grieving, most parents say their emergence into deeper acceptance and peace comes gradually. It's a process with the tangle of emotional changes, not a one-time moment. During these days, months, sometimes years in liminal transition, the wisdom of Jon Kabat-Zinn suggests a stance "What is required is a willingness to look deeply at one's present moments, no matter what they hold, in a spirit of generosity, kindness towards oneself, and openness toward what might be possible."[2]

Four years after the death of her only child, Leah Hanes writes in the *New York Times* of her grief process and growing awareness of the importance of openness. "My heart broke more cruelly and deeply than I thought possible the day my son died. My son's friends are 10 now. A day rarely passes when I don't feel the pain of a child who will always be 6, of motherhood in the past, of bedtime stories read by another while I worked late. No more time, no second chances. I'm still working through my losses, even in my dreams." But she also sees her own growth and understanding changing. "Almost four years later, I know the pain doesn't get better, I just learn, day by day, year by year, to live with it. But this I now know. People we love come, and they frequently go. What matters is staying open; to possibility, to connection, to hope."[3]

Staying open to trusting God's generous grace after losing Krista had been our prayer and challenge early on, but we had no idea where this might lead. Her traumatic death made no sense, yet we wanted to grieve with hope.

Earlier I wrote about when shipwreck moves to "amazement and gladness" when people "land on a new shore." As Sharon Parks writes, "The power of the feeling of shipwreck is located precisely in one's inability to immediately sense the promise of anything beyond the breakup of what has been secure and trustworthy."[4] To lose a child eradicates all future images of family life with this beloved one, forever altering the lives of siblings and parents. As individuals and families, we need to recompose our images of the future.

Just as we need to give attention to grief, we must also figure out a path to living creatively in our future. Most parents acknowledge the value of ordinary ongoing responsibilities of living. Whether caring for other children who still need nurture, working in jobs that demand our talents and commitments, or comforting family and friends who also need our support, daily challenges continue. This often involves a choice of the will, such as creating a healthy dinner or taking a walk whether we feel like it or not. During times when my spirit and energy flag, I find encouragement in the biblical guidance, "Be strong and of good courage; . . . for the Lord your God is with you wherever you go" (Josh. 1:9 RSV). When hard times lead to anxiety, which is common after a sudden death, and the universe seems so random, I appreciate the New Testament reminder that "For God has not given us a spirit of fear, but of power, and of love and of a sound mind" (2 Tim. 1:7 NKJV). By living in the present moment, attentive as possible to the promises of each day, the acute raw pain eventually eases. The great goodness and privilege of life begins to infuse our days again.

"When we survive shipwreck—when we do wash up on a new shore—there is gladness, the gladness of relief and restoration. It is a gladness that pervades one's whole being;

there is a new sense of vitality, be it quiet or exuberant," claims Parks. "Usually, however, there is more than relief and restoration: there is transformation. We discover something different beyond the loss."[5]

During times when my spirit and energy flag, I find encouragement in the biblical guidance, "Be strong and of good courage; . . . for the LORD your God is with you wherever you go."
—*Joshua 1:9 RSV*

Never are we able to replace, to completely recompose, what was before. The loss of a loved one and their meaning in our life is irretrievable; it must be grieved and mourned. "But the gladness is the discovery that life continues to unfold with meaning, with connections of significance and delight," states Parks.[6] "Our joy came back, and we could laugh again and feel gratitude for having had Matthew in our lives," recalls Barbara Hofmaier four years after her son's suicide.

A strong sense of meaning emerges for Mari Bailey when she gives her energy as a volunteer speaker for the Donor Network of Arizona. Several months before her son Michael was shot, she happened to take him for a new driver's license. He mentioned afterward his disappointment in not seeing a way to designate himself as an organ donor. "This was so typical of his generous nature. He'd give homeless people his last coins and people loved him," said Mari. "This fortuitous conversation gave me a clear signal of what his choice would be when doctors gently asked about organ donation, as we faced having to make the decision to take Michael off life support." To her surprise, over 75 recipients benefited, receiving everything from skin for burn victims, corneas, bones, pancreas, liver, kidneys, and more, even though his lungs and heart were too compromised from bullet wounds. In the Arizona program (the Donor Network of

Arizona) where she volunteers, there is a formal process where donors and recipients can exchange contact information if both parties want to do this. "I received a beautiful handwritten letter from a forty-year-old farm mother who received Michael's pancreas. She was so thankful that this gift saved her life. I have also recently been in touch with a Native American woman who received one of Michael's kidneys."

During our early years in liminal space, neither Jim nor I experienced any definite ending of grief. But there were clearly graced moments when we deeply sensed movements toward healing. One happened in California while visiting Yosemite for Jim's research on John Muir. Eager to see the Merced River, we climbed the trail to the headwaters where a large swimming hole drew sunbathers. Playful ouzel birds joined people in soaking up the shimmering sun. As I waded into the center of the "river of mercy," I felt an overwhelming sense of gratitude, aware that Jim and I had been surrounded by mercy in the three years since Krista's death. My heart rested with a profound sense of peace and thankfulness. "What happened out there?" asked Jim. "You seemed so radiantly happy that I took a picture to capture the moment." Jim found similar marker moments, especially when returning to Central and South America with friends. Did it mark an "end" to grief? No way, but these encouraging signposts gave us hope that someday we would wash up on a new shore.

"I liken grief to an intruder who breaks into your house, demands attention, and takes over your life . . . it would never leave. . . . So I invited grief to sit at the table and offered hospitality."
—Jan Skaggs

One defiant and truthful mother told a counselor, "I don't want to find blessings in a broken heart." I assume she may have been responding to friends trying to comfort her with the cliché of "counting one's blessings" too early after a death, before she engaged in grief work. But ultimately, gratitude proves pivotal. Parents tell me they only entered peace and acceptance when they could remember with thankfulness all that the child meant in their life.

Along with gladness, there is also amazement. This is what happens when we look back and say, "I survived that?" Or, as Mary Beth Baker said in gratefulness as she describes the years after Stephen's death, "I hit bottom and it held."

Parents even talk about appreciation for the new growth in their lives that emerges after loss. Sometimes this includes new exterior actions, but they also speak of changes in their interior life. "I liken grief to an intruder who breaks into your house, demands attention and takes over your life," explains Jan Skaggs. "It can feel violent, rude, and socially unacceptable . . . such as when I'd cry at inappropriate places. But in time, I recognized grief was here to stay . . . it would never leave. I'd never be able to go back to the old normal. So I invited grief to sit at the table and offered hospitality. It even became my friend," says Skaggs. "Eventually grief became a tool God used to redecorate and remodel my life, a wrecking crew that led to reconstruction. Grief knocked out walls of assumptions, prejudice, and quick judgment and has rebuilt a much bigger room now . . . more grace filled, more welcoming to others, filled with a lighter heart."

In hearing stories of shipwreck and gladness, I saw how interconnected and inseparable the heart and depth of our loss relates directly to the heart and depth of our love. I began to comprehend how under deep loss for one we love lies a wellspring of love. Wellsprings provide an abundant continual supply. Once we access this underground love we discover a rich power source for healing and creative living. As we repattern the fabric of our days, we face pivotal choices. If we give ourselves time to grieve, allowing ourselves to mourn, and patiently attend to sorrow, we are taking steps to release the pain, hurt, and bewilderment that any death brings. In contrast, if we block facing profound losses and stuff our grief, we place a concrete lid over the wellspring. That closes off the refreshing spring of artesian waters, the abiding memories of one we love that could be embraced for positive nourishment. If we tap into this wellspring of love beneath the sorrow and remember our beloved person with thanksgiving, this resource can inspire us to live abundantly. I like that one of Krista's last journal entries in Bolivia was Psalm 87:7 (NASB), "All my springs of joy are in you." Kahlil Gibran's wisdom becomes our own truth: "The deeper that sorrow carves into your being, the more joy you can contain."[7]

Many parents told me how the death of their child became a crucible moment and, in time, led to surprising new ways of engaging life. In a *Larry King Live* interview with Marilyn Carlson Nelson, cited as one of *U.S. News and World Reports* "best American leaders" and author of *How We Lead Matters: Reflections on a Life of Leadership*,[8] she astutely describes this process in liminal space that led to a vibrant new place in her life. When their nineteen-year-old daughter died in an automobile accident, she recalls the times of anger and depression that first emerged as she and her husband tried to make sense of this "senseless" death.

"As we started to try to come to grips with it, what we were more aware of than anything was that she didn't have any more time. And we had time. And the fact that her life was cut off made us realize that ours could be cut off. Any minute. And we wanted to use our days," says Nelson.[9] Since her daughter's death in 1985, she served as the first female CEO of Carlson, the world's largest global travel business. There she became renowned for the principles of love and care she initiated into a corporate structure.

"I became convinced that I wanted every day to matter. So at night when I go to bed and pull back the covers, I ask myself if I were an artist and today was a painting, would I step back and say, I'd sign my name to that? And some days I can sign my name to . . . I've been loving. I've been forgiving. I've perhaps struck a blow for things that I believe in and haven't walked away. Some days I don't," she said. "But just going through the exercise kind of commits me to trying to use those days to cherish the people I love, to try to make the world a more inclusive place and use her needless death as long as I have breath to make a difference." Nelson clearly draws abundantly from the wellspring of love she will always carry for her daughter.

Now fifteen years since Krista died, we live with moments of this amazement and gladness. Aaron, a member of the Charter Class of Krista Colleagues when he returned to Bolivia, poured his prodigious energy into developing the Krista Foundation, became founding editor of the *Global Citizen Journal*, and now serves on the Board. A few years later he married Gabriela Morena, a beautiful young Bolivian woman who is now the mother of their two children, our heart-grandchildren, Thiago and Ava. Gabriela truly is a blessing in our family, and we've been grateful that she welcomes his former in-laws into their marriage. Aaron returned to the states to attend Harvard's Kennedy School of Government for a Master's degree. At the same time our daughter Susan gave birth to Hunter. Susan and Peter live in Boston, so they were delighted when Gabriela became their nanny while Aaron finished his studies. "She's like family," says Susan, and she truly is. Aaron has become a son to me, especially since he lost his mother, Linda. Jim attended their festive wedding in Santa Cruz, Bolivia, where over a dozen of Aaron's friends flew to celebrate. Aaron continues to travel throughout the world assisting World Vision's mission with impoverished communities.

Jefferson met and married Kris, a wonderful woman, and they live in Coeur d' Alene, Idaho, about an hour away. We assumed they'd not have children of their own since she'd been a single mom raising three teenage daughters. Can you imagine our delight at our fourth of July picnic when they proudly gave us an ultrasound of our future granddaughter, Erin? The international nature of our family grew again when Susan and Peter adopted Quinlen, a merry two-year-old girl from Vietnam. Of course, Jim and I wish our family wasn't so spread out geographically, especially when we see what bonding and enjoyment grandparents and grandchildren experience when living in the same town. Still, our annual "cousins' reunion" with our three families and five grandchildren seems like a miracle. This truly brings the deepest sense of gladness as the circle of life continues.

We share the common invitation of
living with trust and boldness, opening
our hearts so that hope eclipses fear.

The Krista Foundation for Global Citizenship now includes almost 230 Krista Colleagues, spirited young Americans with a similar desire for service as Krista. Their friendships enliven our days and inspire our confidence in the future of American leaders. Whether feasting with seventeen new Krista Colleagues around the Hearth table, seeing older Krista Colleagues leading astute workshops on the ethics of inner-city or international service at our annual conference, or celebrating the first Krista Colleague wedding, gladness abounds.

Having walked these years with sorrow and love mingled together, we truly know the broken heart can expand to embrace both. Laughter, joy, peace, and meaning do come again! There is life after death, even here on earth. When we sing the historic hymn "Great Is Thy Faithfulness" with the refrain "Morning by morning, new mercies I see," these words ring with authenticity. As we encounter so many others with their own losses, a kinship unites us. We share the common invitation of living with trust and boldness, opening our hearts so that hope and love eclipse fear. I long for readers to sense a similar companionship from the candid stories that grieving parents shared for this book.

Still, there isn't a day that goes by without memories of Krista and awareness of her physical absence in our lives. Now the intensity of early sorrow and pain emerges only occasionally. Far more often, there is a deep gratefulness that she abides always in the sweetness of good memories for all she brought to us as a family, for the love she showered on Aaron, her friends, and the world. For this we give thanks.

For all that has been, thanks.
For all that will be, yes.[10]

DISCUSSION GUIDE
FOR PARENTS AND GRIEF GROUPS

Prologue

1. In what ways do you hope this book will be a companion to you, or to those you befriend through the grief journey?
2. Do you agree with Dr. Wolfelt that we are a "mourning-avoidant" culture? If so, where have you sensed this within your community, workplace, or family?
3. Where and with whom have you found your strongest understanding and support?
4. Have you had other life experiences where you have seen the intermingling of joy and sorrow that Gibran mentions?
5. Why do you think the author believes it is important to trust your own imaginative ways for finding strength and healing during loss?

Chapter 1: Attending to a Broken Heart

1. When do you experience moments in your day or week when grief "demands attention"?
2. Does Frankl's belief that we can transcend painful experiences by choosing one's attitude ring true to your own observations and life? Why or why not?
3. Can one really "grow" through suffering? In what ways?
4. Have you found the loss of a loved one raised similar questions to the author's about God's protective hand or other theological issues?

Chapter 2: Finding Solace in Shared Stories

1. In what ways does the description that persons in grief experience an "intense yearning, a sense that part of you is missing" describe your own feelings? Or not?
2. Have you ever felt that talking about the loved one you have lost makes someone too uncomfortable?
3. What more have you learned about your child through someone sharing a story? Was this comforting or distressing?
4. What tangible actions, like making a story quilt, scrapbook, or music collection have you done or someone else done for you that will help keep your child's memory alive?
5. Torvik wrote about her family's Norwegian silences where some believe "if pain is given no voice, it lacks power to harm." What cultural patterns exist in your own family that affect conversations around pain and loss?

Chapter 3: Taking Small Steps Daily

1. In the months after loss, what still seemed "essential" that you continued doing? What were you able to let go?
2. In a typical day now, what is your "next thing"? What small steps have you found useful?

3. If you have experienced other "shipwrecks" in your life, what inner strength and/or wisdom did you draw from that proved helpful?
4. Have you been told "everything will be different after the death of a child"? In what ways does this seem an accurate or inaccurate description of either your "interior" life or your "exterior" actions?

Chapter 4: Trusting Ourselves in the Midst of Grief

1. Are there places, at home or elsewhere, associated with your loved one that are either comforting or painful or both?
2. Is your response to being in these places different from other family members? How have these differences or similarities affected your relationships?
3. Why is trusting one's response in grief important, and sometimes so hard?
4. Do you agree that one of the great enemies of grief is giving oneself a timetable? Have you felt this subtle pressure from others or yourself?

Chapter 5: Allowing Time for the Long Season of Sorrow

1. Has it been possible for you to "dose" the pain? How does this differ from the concern that "distractions" prevent us from facing grief?
2. In what physical ways, if any, has grief affected you? When have you experienced "grief bursts"?
3. Levine believes that if we stay open to mercy, it will help us discover a path to peace. What would "staying open" look like in your own life?
4. "Hope emerges when people make a commitment and intention to heal," according to Wolfelt. What commitments are you making that reflect your intention to heal?

Chapter 6: Receiving Grace along the Journey

1. Have you found any truth in Lamott's assurance that there will be "flecks or nuggets of gold" in your grief journey?
2. Have any surprise opportunities for growth opened for you?
3. Pennye Nixon found meaning in the poem "Kindness" after she lost her daughter. Have there been any writings that have added meaning to your journey?
4. Have you or others had dreams about the one you've lost? Were they helpful or more disturbing?

Chapter 7: Savoring Solitude

1. If you had a desire for some times of solitude, how did you carve this out? Any obstacles?
2. What benefits do you find in having time alone? What difficulties?
3. After Capulli's son died, she found herself hesitant to still have fun in life until friends encouraged her. Have you had similar feelings? What gives you enjoyment and pleasure?
4. If you are married or living in a blended family, what differences have you observed in how you and your spouse, or partner, grieve? Does Doka's description of instrumental and intuitive grievers fit your family?

Chapter 8: Seeking Companions along the Way

1. Grief is seen as internal, the private thoughts and feelings we have when someone we love dies. Have you ever felt that you are to "keep grief to yourself"?
2. Mourning is seen as external, where we find ways to express grief outside of ourselves. What public ways gave you and others a place to express grief?
3. Have there been any groups where you felt comfortable shar-

ing your story? What proved useful in this companionship? Any disappointments?

4. What spiritual resources, insights, and communities offered solace in your pilgrimage? Are there times, like Mari experienced, where theological "answers or advice" felt hurtful?

5. After her son's suicide, Hofmaier recognized that her family was at a crossroad. "We had a choice to make here, whether to keep hope alive." What choices do you imagine for your family?

Chapter 9: Encouraging Creativity to Ease the Pain

1. MacKerrow found that each tree she planted for The Susie Forest gave her a reminder that "life goes on and starts anew." Are there any reminders for you of the continuity of life?

2. Have you discovered any new or renewed creative ways to express your grief?

3. Although the dire divorce statistics predicted after the death of a child proved false, what particular challenges do marriages face in the midst of deep grief?

4. Hunt discovered that she needed to live with love and sorrow always alongside. Could you describe a typical day when you were aware of living with love and sorrow intermingled?

5. Are there moments of extending or receiving hospitality, or creating special meals, that strengthen your spirit?

Chapter 10: Designing Rituals of Meaning

1. Are there any special ways that you or your family remember birthdays or the anniversary of your child's death?

2. Are there any rituals of remembrance that others have done for you to help ease your grief?

3. Are there "habits of the mind" that you find useful or hurtful as you live with grief?
4. What could be the value of creating new rituals around important holidays?
5. Why would many discover that active gratitude provides a valuable practice during difficult times?

Chapter 11: Nurturing Hope in Nature

1. Are there any places in nature that are meaningful in remembering your loved one?
2. Where or to whom have you gone to explore your spiritual questions?
3. In O'Rourke's research on grief, she concludes "Nor does a belief in a heavenly reunion protect you from grief." How has your belief or lack of belief in an afterlife shaped your grief?
4. Have you had any experiences in nature that gave you a greater peace after loss?

Chapter 12: Discovering the Healing Power of Forgiveness

1. Why might Skaggs believe "Forgiveness is a gift we give ourselves"?
2. Is there someone you sense needs forgiveness around the death of your child? Yourself? Another?
3. "Forgiveness is a process that happens over time, not instantly," believes Egolf. When might Smedes's concern that forgiveness can happen too soon be valid?
4. "It's [forgiveness] your move," states another. Is forgiveness a choice? An action? An attitude?

ORGANIZATIONS AND SUPPORT GROUPS FOR BEREAVED PARENTS

MANY OF THESE ORGANIZATIONS HAVE LOCAL CHAPTERS, PLUS A STRONG INTERNET PRESENCE.

⚜

Alliance of Hope for Suicide Survivors
Online forum and Web site
www.allianceofhope.org

American Childhood Cancer Organization (ACCO)
(formerly Candlelighters Childhood Cancer)
10920 Connecticut Ave., Suite A
Kensington, MD 20895
855–858–2226 or 301–962–3520
www.acco.org

Beareaved Parents of the USA (includes Spanish-language site)
P.O. Box 662
St. Peters, MO 63376
800–273–8255
www.bereavedparentsusa.org

The Compassionate Friends
P.O. Box 3696
Oak Brook, IL 60522
630–990–0010 or 877–969–0010
www.compassionatefriends.org

First Candle/SIDS Alliance
2105 Laurel Bush Rd., Suite 201
Bel Air, MD 21015
800–221–7437 or 443–640–1049
www.firstcandle.org

Loving Outreach to Survivors of Suicide (LOSS)
721 N. LaSalle St.
Chicago, IL 60654
312–655–7283
www.catholiccharities.net/loss

MISS Foundation (includes Spanish-language site)
77 E. Thomas Rd., Suite 112
Phoenix, AZ 85012
888–455–MISS or 602–279–MISS
www.missfoundation.org
This foundation includes strong focus on infant and toddler death and advocacy.

Mothers Against Drunk Driving (MADD)
511 E. John Carpenter Freeway
Suite 700
Irving, TX 75062
877–623–3435
www.MADD.org

Parents of Murdered Children
4960 Ridge Ave., Suite 2
Cincinnati, OH 45209
513–721–5683 or 888–818–POMC
www.pomc.com

TAPS: Tragedy Assistance Program for Survivors
3033 Wilson Blvd., Suite 630
Arlington, VA 22201
800–959–8277
taps.org
For families grieving the death of a loved one in military service

ACKNOWLEDGMENTS

*One can only see by loving; love makes all
things visible and all labor light.*

THESE THOUGHTS FROM ENVIRONMENTALIST JOHN MUIR ECHO
my experiences during the past nine years of research and
interviews for *Pilgrimage through Loss*. One could imagine that
writing a book focusing on parents who have lost children
might be discouraging, only filled with sorrow. But, in fact,
coming to know families who shared the wellspring of visible
love for their child often inspired me. Their vibrant courage,
as they live their days entwined with sorrow and love, demonstrated the depth of human strength and resilience. Love for a
child never ends.

I am grateful for each of the fathers, mothers, grandparents,
brothers, and sisters who welcomed me into their hearts, often
with the hope that their story might comfort another grieving
parent. Mari Bailey, Sarah Bain, Mary Beth and Dick Baker,
Meredith Banka, Sheree Capulli, Sharon Clegg, Babs Egolf,
Shelly Fry, George and Lila Girvin, Diana Graham, Barbara
Grigsby, Diana Hartvigsen, Cheryl Hillis, Barbara Hofmaier,

Laurie Horn, Jim Hunt, Carol Koller, Shelly Kuney, Patty McClary, Steve Nelson, Pennye Nixon, John Perkins, Lori Kuney Sawyer, Jerry Sittser, Jan and Harold Skaggs, and Mark Terrell told stories of living with great heartbreak, but also daily courage, renewal, even joy. They enliven these pages with their truths and wisdom.

Jim and I will always treasure our son-in-law Aaron Ausland's honest expressions of bewilderment as a grieving young husband while he wrestled with anger, theological questions, forgiveness, and faith-filled living amid facing such loss. His writings and presentations to the Krista Foundation community on his pilgrimage, now included here, allow others to name and also wrestle with the paradoxes of living.

Early readers offered candid critique and didn't let the loss of Krista keep them from important suggestions for revisions. Shirley Ferris, Jane Kirkpatrick, Judy Palpant, Pamela Corpran Parker, Kathy Peterson, Mardelle Shagool, Ronald White, plus several of the parents interviewed all improved the initial drafts.

For several years, Karlene Arguinchona, a medical emergency room doctor offered a grief group for mothers in her home and provided valuable metaphors on healing. Gloria Nielsen, a former hospital chaplain who leads bereavement groups at First Presbyterian Church, gave of her knowledge, donated many books, and connected me with some parents for interviews.

Jim and I will always be thankful that the Mennonite Central Committee, the organization that Krista and Aaron volunteered with, provided us the important trip to Bolivia. This visible experience allowed us to meet the indigenous families in the Bañado de la Cruz village where Krista hoped to show "God's love through actions." The generous actions of the women's cooperative, which prepared a feast and shared private dreams and their love for Krista and Aaron, will live forever in our hearts. We are humbled by the chance encounter with the mystery Quechua angel of grace, who broke bread with Jim on the bus from Machu Pichu after sharing her similar loss of a twenty-five-year-old daughter. Her kind gesture connected us to parental love and loss that knows no international boundaries.

The many poets who craft words with such care spoke to me and to many of the parents I interviewed. Leonard Cohen, Mark Doty, Jeremy Funk, Jim Hunt, Kahlil Gibran, Denise Lassaw, Namomi Shihad Nye, John O'Donohue, Mary Oliver, and Theodore Roetke gave meaning when we were wordless. Richard Niebuhr's ideas of "shipwreck and gladness" introduced to me by Sharon Daloz Parks in her original book *The Critical Years* offered an important metaphor, as did Moses Pulei's Masai practice of sharing stories as the greatest gift one gives to another in grief.

A book often has many midwives, and a special thanks goes to Judi Bergen, Valerie Norwood, and Dorothy and Martha Longbrake for their serendipitous part in bringing this book to fruition, and to Jana Riess for her insightful understanding of parents' needs. Throughout this journey, my agent, Roy M. Carlisle, has invested his considerable energy, talent, editorial skill, and belief in *Pilgrimage through Loss*. His encouragement and friendship prove invaluable. The excellent editorial leadership of David Dobson and the Westminster John Knox Press staff clearly enhanced my initial manuscript.

But it is our living family, "that which is close at hand," who have given continued meaning, fun, and joy. Grandchildren Hunter, Quinlen, Erin, Thiago, and Ava especially keep our spirits focused forward. My husband Jim's daily companionship, adventuresome spirit, writing feedback, and faithful determination to live boldly with love and sorrow have been the finest gifts in my life. Grief shared truly is grief halved.

PERMISSIONS

NOTES

Prologue

1. Elisabeth Kübler-Ross, *On Death and Dying* (New York: Scribner, 1967).

2. Elisabeth Kübler-Ross, *On Grief and Grieving: Finding the Meaning of Grief through the Five Stages of Loss* (New York: Scribner, 2005).

3. Meghan O'Rourke, "Good Grief," *New Yorker*, February 1, 2010.

4. Kahlil Gibran, "On Joy and Sorrow," *The Prophet* (New York: Knopf, 1973), 29.

5. Alan Wolfelt, *Understanding Your Grief* (Fort Collins, CO: Companion Press, 2004).

Chapter 1: Attending to a Broken Heart

1. Victor Frankl, *Man's Search for Meaning* (Boston: Beacon Press, 2006), 75.

2. Ibid., 76.

3. Gerald Sittser, *A Grace Disguised: How the Soul Grows through Grief* (Grand Rapids: Zondervan, 1997).

4. Anne McCracken and Mary Semel, *A Broken Heart Still Beats: After Your Child Dies* (Center City, MN: Hazelden, 1998), xxvii.

5. Mark Epstein, "The Trauma of Being Alive," *The New York Times*, August 3, 2013, SR8.

Chapter 2: Finding Solace in Shared Stories

1. Solveig Torvik, *Nikolai's Fortune* (Seattle: University of Washington Press, 2005), xiv.
2. Jeremy Funk, "Joy Dance," *Global Citizen Journal: A Journal for Young Adults Engaging the World through Service* 5 (2010): 6.

Chapter 3: Taking Small Steps Daily

1. Sharon Daloz Parks, *Big Questions, Worthy Dreams: Mentoring Emerging Adults in Their Search for Meaning, Purpose, and Faith*, rev. ed. (San Francisco: Jossey-Bass, 2011), 24–26.
2. Robert Maurer, *The Kaizen Way: One Small Step Can Change Your Life* (New York: Workman Publishing, 2004), 8.

Chapter 4: Trusting Ourselves in the Midst of Grief

1. Ann Morrow Lindberg, *Hour of Gold, Hour of Lead: Diaries and Letters of Ann Morrow Lindbergh 1929–1932* (New York: Harcourt, Brace, and Co., 1973), 292.

Chapter 5: Allowing Time for the Long Season of Sorrow

1. William Stafford, "Consolations," in *The Darkness around Us Is Deep: Selected Poems* (New York: Harper Perennial, 1994), 6.
2. Stephen Levine, *Unattended Sorrow: Recovering from Loss and Reviving the Heart* (New York: Rodale Books, 2006), 6.
3. Nicholas Wolterstorff, *Lament for a Son* (Grand Rapids: Eerdmans Publishing Co., 1987), 54.
4. Ibid., 5.
5. Alan Wolfelt, *Understanding Your Grief* (Fort Collins, CO: Companion Press, 2004), 13.

Chapter 6: Receiving Grace along the Journey

1. Naomi Shihab Nye, "Kindness," in *The Words under the Words* (Portland, OR: Eighth Mountain Press, 1995), 42.
2. Mark Doty, *Heaven's Coast: A Memoir* (New York: Harper Perennial, 1997), 287.

Chapter 7: Savoring Solitude

1. "Kathryn Tyler, "Giving Time to Grieve," www.kathryntyler .com/giving_time_to_grieve.htm, accessed August 10, 2013.
2. Isabel Allende, *The Sum of Our Days: A Memoir* (New York: Harper, 2008), 114.
3. Isak Dinesen, *Out of Africa* (New York: Modern Library, 1992), 265–66.
4. Denise Lassaw, "Impermanence," in *Whispered Secrets* (Anchorage, AK: Sedna Press, 1991), 39.
5. John O'Donohue, "Beannact," in *Anam Cara: A Book of Celtic Wisdom* (New York: HarperCollins, 1997), v.
6. Kenneth Doka and Terry L. Martin, *Grieving beyond Gender: Understanding the Ways Men and Women Mourn* (New York: Routledge, 2010).
7. Rebecca Nappi, "A Father's Crusade," *The Spokesman Review*, June 17, 2012, D1.
8. Cindy Hval, "Mead Treehouse Pays Tribute to Sister's Vitality," *The Spokesman Review*, October 18, 2012, S1, 11.
9. Christine Clarridge, "Mother Finds Peace, Way to Give Back," *Seattle Times*, March 21, 2008, 1.

Chapter 8: Seeking Companions along the Way

1. Ann McCracken and Mary Semel, *The Broken Heart Still Beats* (Center City, MN: Hazelden Publishing, 2000), 218.
2. Rebecca Nappi, "Never Forgotten," *The Spokesman Review*, May 29, 2011, D7.
3. Mark and Terri Charbonneau, "In Memoriam," *Spokesman Review*, September 19, 2011, B7.
4. Theodore Roethke, "The Far Field," *The Far Field* (New York: Doubleday & Co., 1964), 195.
5. James B. Hunt, "Quecha Dama," *The Global Citizen: A Journal for Young Adults Engaging the World in Service* 1 (Spring 2004): 49.

Chapter 9: Encouraging Creativity to Ease the Pain

1. "Be Thankful: Four Stories of Grateful Giving," *Cooking Light*, December, 2011, 58.
2. Jennifer Larue, "Working to Bring Healing through Art Expression," *The Spokesman Review*, November 4, 2010, N5.
3. "Only 16% of Beareaved Parents Divorce" (2006 Survey),

Compassionate Friends, http://www.compassionatefriends.org/pdf/When_a_Child_Dies-2006_Final.pdf, accessed October 10, 2012.

4. Brendan O'Malley, *Celtic Blessings and Prayers: Making All Things Sacred* (Mystic, CT: Twenty-Third Publications, 1999), 55.

Chapter 10: Designing Rituals of Meaning

1. Nancy Berns, *Closure: The Rush to End Grief and What It Costs Us* (Philadelphia: Temple University Press, 2011), x.

2. Ibid., 169.

3. Ibid., 3.

4. Anna Quindlen, "Public and Private: Life after Death," *New York Times*, May 4, 1994.

5. Kathie Kobler, Rana Limbo, Karen Kavanaugh, "Meaningful Moments—The Use of Ritual in Perinatal and Pediatric Death," *American Journal of Maternal/Child Nursing* 32, no. 5 (October 2007): 288–95.

6. Leonard Cohen, "Anthem," in *Stranger Music: Selected Poems and Lyrics* (Toronto: McClelland & Stewart, Inc., 1993), 373.

Chapter 11: Nurturing Hope in Nature

1. Rachel Carson, www.great-quotes.com/quotes/102413.

2. Meghan O'Rourke, "Good Grief," *New Yorker*, February 1, 2010.

3. Kathleen Dean Moore, *Wild Comfort: The Solace of Nature* (Boston: Trumpeter, 2010), ix.

4. Matthew Fox, *Original Blessing: A Primer in Creation Spirituality* (Rochester, VT: Bear & Co., 1983), 68.

5. Mary Oliver, *Why I Wake Early: New Poems* (Boston: Beacon Press, 2004), 3.

Chapter 12: Discovering the Healing Power of Forgiveness

1. Lewis B. Smedes, *The Art of Forgiving: When You Need to Forgive and Don't Know How* (New York: Ballentine Books, 1996), 137.

2. Martin Luther King Jr., *Strength to Love* (Minneapolis: Fortress Press, 1981), 95.

Conclusion: Doorway into Thanks

1. Roger Rosenblath quoted in Donna Rifkind, "Turning toward the Shore," *New York Times,* January 8, 2012, 9.

2. Jon Kabat Zinn, www.usguu.org/profiles/blogs/kent-trumpet -june-2012, May 22, 2012, accessed August 10, 2013.

3. Leah Hanes, "Modern Love: Gifts for the Broken Hearted," *New York Times,* October 15, 2010, ST8.

4. Sharon Parks, *The Critical Years* (San Francisco: Harper & Row, 1986), 25.

5. Sharon Daloz Parks, *Big Questions, Worthy Dreams: Mentoring Emerging Adults in Their Search for Meaning, Purpose, and Faith,* rev. ed. (San Francisco: Jossey Bass, 2011), 25.

6. Ibid.

7. Kahlil Gibran, *The Prophet* (New York: Alfred A Knopf, 1923), 29.

8. Marilyn Carlson Nelson, *How We Lead Matters: Reflections on a Life of Leadership* (New York: McGraw Hill, 2008).

9. Marilyn Carlson Nelson, *Larry King Live Interview*, November 7, 2010.

10. Dag Hammarskjold, *Markings* (New York: Random House/ Vintage Books, 2006), 89.

ABOUT THE AUTHOR

LINDA LAWRENCE HUNT IS A TEACHER, SPEAKER, SCHOLAR, AND author. A professor of English at Whitworth University where she served as Director of Writing, she also helped initiate their innovative Service-Learning and Writing across the Curriculum programs. After their twenty-five-year-old daughter died while volunteering with her husband in Bolivia, Linda and her husband, Jim, a history professor at Whitworth, cofounded the Krista Foundation for Global Citizenship (www.krista foundation.org). She left teaching to develop the Krista Foundation and continue her freelance writing career and is a member of the American Society of Journalists and Authors.

Linda has authored or coauthored five books and is the author of the best-selling *Bold Spirit: Helga Estby's Forgotten Walk across Victorian America*. It was honored with the Pacific Northwest Booksellers Award, the Washington State Book award, and the national Willa Cather award for nonfiction (www.boldspiritacrossamerica.com).

Since the publication of *Bold Spirit*, Linda has keynoted over two hundred speaking engagements in the United States, Norway, and Germany, including academic environments (Princeton and Fuller Seminary, St. Olaf University, New York University, and the Claremont Graduate School); spoke at civic and community organizations across America, such as the Norwegian Embassy sponsored by the Smithsonian, American Association of University Women, libraries, museums, historical societies, bookstores, and church luncheons and retreats for many denominations; and given international presentations at Martin Luther Universität Halle–Wittenberg, Check Point Charlie Foundation in Berlin and the national Norwegian library in Oslo.

Linda holds a BA from the University of Washington and a PhD from Gonzaga University. Linda and Jim live in Spokane, Washington, where their guest center, the Hearth, and global gardens provide a gathering place for creative renewal.

CPSIA information can be obtained at www.ICGtesting.com
Printed in the USA
LVOW11s0025050214

372334LV00004B/261/P